MW00744801

Solving
the Mystery
of the
Smiling Church

By Peter Carver Johnson
"Smiling Pete"

Illustrated By Jim Reidy

This book presents the opinions of Peter C. Johnson,
Member of Evelyn S. Johnson LLC,
Doing business as P E Carver Company,
Concord, New Hampshire 03302

www.pecarver.com
www.smilingpete.com

Solving the Mystery of the Smiling Church
Published by Evelyn S. Johnson LLC, DBA P E Carver Co,
Concord, New Hampshire 03302

Copyright © 2008 by Peter Carver Johnson

All Rights Reserved.

Library of Congress Cataloging-in-Publication Data

ISBN 978-0-615-18673-3

Scripture quotations are from the Revised Standard Version
of the Bible, copyright © 1946, 1952, and 1971 by the National Council of
the Churches of Christ in the USA.
Used by permission. All rights reserved.

For more information, contact P E Carver Co., P.O. Box 4112, Concord, NH 03302

www.pecarver.com
www.smilingpete.com

Technical Credits

Front Cover Design	FATACT Graphics, LLC
Inside Layout	FATACT Graphics, LLC www.fatactgraphics.com
Back Cover Design & Cover Layout	Hoik Advertising hoik@verizon.net
Picture of Smiling Pete In the Garden with Jesus	Evelyn S. Johnson

---

The Great Commission Help Center

Assisting Bible-Believing Churches In Fulfilling The Great Commission

Please visit us on the Web at:

www.gchcenter.com
or
www.smilingpete.com

TABLE OF CONTENTS

Go

This book is about the "Great Commission." I wrote it in response to a calling from God to address the mystery of how churches can grow by effectively reaching out to the lost and making disciples of Christ.

This book should also help individual Christians with their work, walk, and witness as they serve the Lord in the "Great Commission." The book is formatted in sections, most of which answer questions that I am frequently asked.

Jesus wants all Bible-believing churches to learn to hear His voice, to rely on Him, and to go with surrendered hearts and hands to do the Father's work.

This book is designed to be a tool to help guide church leaders and members through the process of fulfilling the Great Commission, and to provide solutions to problems that arise along the way.

It is my prayer that you will serve Him, the God of Jacob, with an undivided heart, experience the fullness of His love, and realize that the Truth is a person. May we someday meet along the road in life, and share His love together.

Matthew 28:19-20 commands, "Go therefore and make disciples of all nations, baptizing them in the name of the Father and of the Son and of the Holy Spirit, teaching them to observe all that I have commanded you; and lo, I am with you always, to the close of the age."

In the Beginning

On a cloudy summer day in 1962, I clearly remember standing in the driveway, lying to my mother, and sneaking off to have my first cigarette. It was out behind the barn, crouched beside a big pile of cow manure, that the Devil took my hand. I was fourteen years old.

Later, at twenty-nine, after fifteen years of yielding to the devil's temptations of hollow pleasures and self-fulfillment, and enduring the pain and misery that followed, I wanted out. I became a seeker.

The Lord sent two couples from Pascagoula, Mississippi to tell me the salvation story, and lead me to Him. I confessed I was a sinner, accepted Jesus as my Lord and Savior, and was born again.

The Mystery

He immediately began transforming me and within a few months, revealed that His purpose for my life was to help churches and individuals fulfill the "Great Commission."

The last twenty-nine years have been very active with working, listening, learning, praying, studying the Bible, going to school, and asking a lot of questions.

After several years of working with many churches on outreaches, evangelism projects of all kinds, and growth follow-up studies, the Mystery emerged.

I had been blessed with a mentor who had been trained in evangelism-based church growth. He took over as pastor of a local church with a handful of people. The church grew. Boy, did it grow! Soon, it seemed like each and every week, at least one soul accepted Christ as their Lord and Savior. These new people were then baptized, taught about the Kingdom of God, introduced to the Bible, helped to discover their spiritual gifts, and encouraged in their service to the

Lord. Each one of them joined a small group that helped put their gifts to good use. They became part of the cycle of joy, peace, and love. This was truly a "Smiling Church" or "the most fun in town."

The Lord led me to other churches and other projects, and taught me about different types of growth programs; but I was increasingly consumed with this Mystery: Why do some churches succeed in regularly adding converts, while others rarely or never do so?

That night I got down on my knees and talked to my Savior for a long time. I expressed my frustrations and questions one-by-one, and lifted them up to Him. Three days later I heard from Him in a way I hadn't expected.

Hidden Scrolls

It was about 4:30 one morning when He spoke to me. It was one of the most startling experiences of my life. He said, "NOTHING!" I was immediately on my knees beside the bed. He gave me a scripture, John 15:5, which reads, "I am the vine, you are the branches. He who abides in me and I in him, he it is that bears much fruit, for apart from me you can do nothing."

Before I knew it, I was on my way to work and found myself in front of an office supply store. I ran in and bought a dictionary just to make sure I understood the exact meaning of the word 'nothing.'

Since then, a steady stream of knowledge has opened up to me. I go to my Savior constantly. All is well. I have absolute confidence and trust in the wisdom and guidance He gives me, and answers to the basic Mystery come as needed. It's all about Him...not me.

I had written an earlier, much shorter version of this book during a period of great frustration when I began to realize that a strong emphasis on home groups is a big part of church growth, but at that time didn't understand how everything fit together. However, just prior to publication, I started getting strangely ill. My temperature began to rise slightly higher every two or three days. Then came a persistent headache and it was painful to move my eyes and look around. Next I experienced constant fatigue, balance and motion problems, and other symptoms. The book sat on my desk and in the computer. Looking back, I now realize that I needed to listen to God much more before proceeding with publication. God wanted my solution to be correct and complete.

A lot of time was spent with doctors. Months passed. I got sicker. Finally, early one Sunday morning, my wife Evelyn helped me into the car and we went to a new emergency room in town. The young doctor took one look at me and told me that I had Rocky Mountain Spotted Fever. She said that an infected tick had bitten me. It seems that there are three types of similar infections that a tick can carry, which have the same basic effect. The most commonly known is  Rocky Mountain Spotted Fever. She said that it didn't matter which one I had, they all could be treated with the same antibiotic. The medicine started a long, hard recovery. During the first few weeks I was worried that a lot of the effects of the disease would never go away. The fever gradually subsided but a lot of the other symptoms lingered on.

Instead of traveling, I stayed close to home during the healing process and visited several churches in town. I realized that God was drawing me to one church in particular that I had visited previously. Although the church was relatively new, the attendance was already a little over three hundred people.

After a couple of months I joined a journaling group led by Pastor Peter Shepherd, the associate pastor of the church. My attitude started changing. Although still a bit confused from the illness, I started realizing that I didn't have all the answers. I thought that just because I had been called to guide churches to fulfill the Great Commission, I knew everything. Wrong. The book stayed on hold during this period while the Lord orchestrated a badly needed ego adjustment. This began a humbling experience as I learned from Pastor Shepherd and learned to really listen to the Lord. He also taught me patience, which caused me to put the book on permanent hold until I learned what I needed to learn. At the same time, it dawned on me that the church was continually growing.

It was time to pay attention to exactly what was going on with this church. I joined a home group. The members of the group prayed for me to be healed. The next morning I felt different. I couldn't believe it. My motion problems were healed and my balance was definitely better! My attitude changed more and I was humbled again. This little group of obedient, faithful believers knew far more than I did about simply trusting the Lord.

God evidently decided that I was headed in the right direction, and He gradually blessed me with the knowledge I needed to complete this book. He has given me a blueprint to help churches make changes in order to fulfill the Great Commission. I certainly don't know all the answers. I still need His mighty hand each day.

After about a year had passed since my initial visit to my new church I noticed that Sunday attendance was now over seven hundred. One Sunday I counted as eleven souls accepted the Lord into their hearts. Another Sunday it was five, and another it was over twenty. I didn't count them all because I was too excited.

The Lord had placed me in this particular church for many reasons. I constantly learned as He spoke through the pastors, quite often through Senior Pastor Peter Bonanno. One Sunday morning Pastor Bonanno was preaching the third part of a four-part series on spiritual warfare. In the Spiritual Warfare section of this book are details of the sermon. He talked about Acts 19:11-20 and how believers had been secretly practicing magic. They had hidden their magic scrolls figuring that God wouldn't find out about their evil practices. He showed us that when we as believers fear God and confess our sins, the enemy of our soul runs away. Also, when believers fear God, word spreads about Jesus, and He is exalted.

The pastor then challenged us. What are our 'Hidden Scrolls?' What evil, what sin, what do we have hidden from the Lord in our lives? Fear of God is a very big factor in church growth. When we fear and respect our Maker and invite Him into all our secret places openly confessing our sins, we can continually move forward serving Him and doing His work. Two weeks later, I was still shaken—and still finding scrolls.

The Solution

Churches that grow by adding new converts exhibit essential characteristics that I call the Determinants of Great Commission Success. They are:

1. **Fear God**

   Respect and fear of Almighty God is an absolute that is sadly misunderstood. Proverbs 1:7 states, "The fear of the Lord is the beginning of knowledge; fools despise wisdom and instruction." He is Omnipotent. He is the One Supreme Being that is above all else. He created all that is created, and deserves ultimate and proper fear and respect that should be instilled in the hearts of men. Too many take liberties that fall short of this respect and there are people who mock Him and His Word. I have known ministers that reject portions of His Word because they choose to ignore descriptions of actions they like to commit that God says will separate them from Him. Psalm 94:11 states, "The Lord, knows the thoughts of man." God clearly knows the motives of man, and is well aware of those who choose not to fear and respect Him.

   He has given us life, and offers eternal life with Him for all who accept the sacrifice He endured for mankind. Our Father and everything He is and has done should not be taken lightly, but should be revered and praised! He will bless those who exalt Him. Acts 9:31 tells us, "So the church throughout all Judea and Galilee and Samar'ia had peace and was built up; and walking in the fear of the Lord and in the comfort of the Holy Spirit it was multiplied."

   Please study Deuteronomy, chapters 28 through 30.

2. **Love God**

   You were created to have a personal relationship with God. He loved you while you were yet His enemy. He has patiently waited for you to accept His Son, to be born again, and walk with Him. The more you get to know Him and His ways, the more you will love, trust, and desire to serve Him. Those who learn to surrender their will to Him whole-heartedly and are the most malleable, receive the peace, joy, and fulfillment in His work that comes with loving and obeying Him. Your witness is a measure of your success. The more you walk in His ways, and get to know Him, the more you will show His love in speech and action. Mark 12:28-31 states, "And one of the scribes came up and heard them disputing with one another, and seeing that he answered them well, asked him, 'Which commandment is the first of all?' Jesus answered, 'The first is, 'Hear, O Israel: The Lord our God, the Lord is one; and you shall love the Lord your God with all your heart, and with all your soul, and with all your mind, and with all your strength.' The second is this, 'You shall love your neighbor as yourself.' There is no other commandment greater than these."

   I have only had a few brief conversations with the senior pastor in my new church, yet I know exactly where he is, and what he is doing most of the time. He is on planet Earth and he is inspiring, motivating, teaching, and equipping people to love and serve God. Rather than try to control a flock, and tell them what to do, he helps them understand how to have a close, loving relationship with their Maker. Our pastors and the other church leaders are unified in providing the venues, support, and encouragement for us to effectively go and love our neighbors in our communities, and elsewhere in the world.

It touches our Father's heart with love each time we listen to Jesus and minister to the poor and needy. It is the very nature of a successful church and a successful Christian to invest a portion of time [which He has given us] and money [which He also provides], representing Him with our hands and hearts. It is simply the nature of love.

It pleases the Lord to use our body of love to have baptisms on a regular basis. The pastors have classes for new Christians and explain the Biblical foundation for baptism in detail. Each person is offered a chance to give their testimony on the day of their baptism. It makes one's heart soar like an eagle to hear these testimonies. Did I mention that our church is the most fun in town?

3. **Consult Jesus**

Jesus must be consulted about everything that you do. Living according to John 15:5 is another absolute. You cannot bear fruit without His direction. The Great Commission is under His command. We must listen to Jesus to understand where our Father is working, and we are to go and join Him in His work. Take a look at John 5:19-20, which says, "Jesus said to them, 'Truly, truly, I say to you, the Son can do nothing of his own accord, but only what he sees the Father doing; for whatever he does, that the Son does likewise. For the Father loves the Son, and shows him all that he himself is doing; and greater works than these will he show him, that you may marvel.' " Now look at John 6:28-29, which reads, "Then they said to him, 'What must we do, to be doing the work of God?' Jesus answered them, 'This is the work of God, that you believe in him whom he has sent.' " Almighty God created this universe in order to glorify His Son. The human mind is incapable of understanding the incredible power that God possesses.

Those that are drawn to Jesus by the Father can come to Him by this work that we do. In these last days we are commanded to be followers of Jesus as He sends us to do this work, the Great Commission. We are to go and love in a hostile world, and we are to make disciples of Christ. Smiling is an obvious part of our church activity because our constant victories in Jesus cause us to smile!

We Christians are being watched and judged by those who are of the world to see if we truly love. We have to be careful to imitate our Savior as we represent Him.

4. **Have Unity**

The leaders must be unified, and the congregation must be unified behind the leaders. From Psalm 133, "Behold, how good and pleasant it is when brothers dwell in unity! It is like the precious oil upon the head, running down upon the beard, upon the beard of Aaron, running down on the collar of his robes! It is like the dew of Hermon, which falls on the mountains of Zion! For there the Lord has commanded the blessing, life for evermore."

You can't move forward in the Great Commission without unity. Leaders must get confirmation of unity by way of encouragement and action from the body. The congregation must get encouragement from the leaders as each parishioner learns to use his or her spiritual gifts to be part of a church that is unified to go and love, all having jobs that strengthen the work. Some have jobs that are functions of in-church activity, while others have jobs that cause them to be sent. Please study the fourth chapter of Ephesians.

It has been my experience that reaching out to the lost is most effective, and unity is easier to achieve and maintain, when a church is committed to developing properly run home groups that multiply. The more united souls you have participating in these groups of love, the more involved you and your church will be in the Great Commission.

5. **Identify Attacks From Your Enemy**

Leaders must learn to identify attacks from Satan and become skilled in conducting spiritual warfare. It is my opinion that the devil will attack everyone in your church, and he will do it often. Please read and study the **Spiritual Warfare** section of this book, and stick together as you learn to be a fighting unit. Don't forget, Satan is a spirit and is constantly roaming through the earth (See I Peter 5:8). He, in his craft, will steal, kill, and destroy. Disrupting your work is very important to him. Mark 4:15 states, "Some people are like seed along the path, where the word is sown. As soon as they hear it, Satan comes and takes away the word that was sown in them." As well as stealing souls and destroying them, he will also try to destroy your unity. Learn to have victory in Christ and defeat the devil!

6. **Praise God With Music**

Music is very important to our God. References to praising Him in song are woven through the Bible like a beautiful tapestry. Exodus 15:1-2 states, "Then Moses and the Israelites sang this song to the Lord: 'I will sing to the Lord, for he is highly exalted. The horse and the rider he has hurled into the sea. The Lord is my strength and my song; he has become my salvation. He is my God, and I will praise him, my father's God, and I will exalt him.' " If you read First and Second Chronicles, Ezra, and Nehemiah you will see that the Lord took special care to separate and provide for the singers and musicians. Likewise, we should extend special care toward the Lord's singers and musicians. Let Him raise up and call a qualified, gifted person that has a heart to be the leader of music in your church. I believe in constantly expanding worship teams, however, there are occasional exceptions to this rule.

I always recommend paying careful attention to the loudness of all amplified sound (from music to message) in any church. I talked to a friend, who is a doctor, the other day, and he agrees with me that many churches send people away by mismanaging sound. Too often, excessively high volume can cause people's ears to ring and may even contribute to permanent hearing damage. I have experienced some services in which the sound was too soft, and some that had distortion through the entire service. Let your praises be controlled in volume and quality, and humble and transparent in heartfelt enthusiasm.

7. Have Sensitivity

We are to reach out into our community to serve and love. We have to be sensitive to the needs of the people we are serving as we do the Father's work. We are commanded to actively share our faith in Christ with a dying world, and make disciples of Christ. We are led to draw people of all walks of life into the Kingdom of God. As they come and visit our church we have to be very sensitive concerning who they are and where they have come from. We also have to be sensitive to minimize any confusion or feelings of strangeness they might experience during their first few visits and to maximize their comfort. One last area we have to be sensitive in is the walk of a new Christian. Each of us is at a different place, and stage in our relationship with God, and in the transforming process we are going through. Not one of us is perfect. All of us have sins that we do battle with and gradually chip away at one-by-one. The important consideration is where one's heart is.

I believe that when these seven Determinants become habits, the church will continually grow, move forward, and become fruitful.

Working Principles...

The past thirty-four years of experience in the business world have reinforced what I was taught in management courses and in college: there are usually five overriding working principles which are unique to each type or phase of business and should be applied in order to achieve success. The better you hone your skills in each of these principles, the more successful you will become. For instance, in sales we were taught that the five rules are: pre-approach, approach, presentation, close, and follow-up. Another example could be the restaurant business. A properly run restaurant might have the operating principles of: good food, right price, good service, cleanliness, and right décor. After the Lord gave me the seven Determinants of Success, I went over the list again and again trying to glean the five principles for successful churches.

I wasted weeks going back over the determinants, buzzing back and forth through the New Testament, looking at Deuteronomy, reading reference books, and getting frustrated. One morning I woke up and felt really stupid. I had been repeating an old habit. I was trying to solve the problem by myself. I got down on my knees to consult my Savior, and surrendered the situation to Him. A couple of days later, I was on my way to Ossipee, New Hampshire and the Holy Spirit told me that it was time, so I pulled the car over and picked up a pen and note pad. God gave me three [not five] working principles for a properly run church. The first principle is in itself all guiding and encompassing, and is the source from which the other two derive. The three principles are: **Love God**, **Love Man**, and **Make Disciples**.

We are not on this planet by accident. He created each of us with the intention and capacity to love and obey God. Together, we are to glorify the Lamb with our witness and work, and our daily walk with Him. He wants us all to be part of a church that marches forward and boldly proclaims our faith. I don't believe in evangelism programs in a church. I believe that each church should be an evangelism organism doing their work here on earth. I believe that most souls come to Jesus by a three-part process. First: they are drawn to Him, second: they are affected by love, and third: they hear and see how God has changed peoples' lives. Ongoing community outreaches and missions to other communities are just natural functions of a church body.

It is my opinion that churches that begin implementing these Growth Determinants will see people rise up through a calling from God and participate in a ministry within your church to go and love. It may involve helping homeless people. It may involve helping the elderly or infirm by cleaning floors, washing windows, shopping, or performing some other act of love. Perhaps you could ask a family with a disabled member to teach you how to help them. The Lord may put a very unique ministry on someone's heart that fulfills a special need in your community, and other church members will get involved as Jesus draws them to it.

One of my pastor friends is trying to start a day care in his church. I've heard of churches that provide free oil changes for the poor, or teams that go to foreign countries and help build houses. God assembles a flock with skills and imagination. It is amazing what can happen when these skills are encouraged, organized, and mobilized. To me, these works of love are forms of evangelism (the winning or revival of personal commitments to Christ). Evangelism is also the love that surrounds souls within the daily and weekly functions inside a church, a place where visitors feel comfortable and valued. Many churches also have special events to which they invite their community. Some even send traveling bands to sing to the incarcerated. They will know you by your love and witness.

A church is useless if sharing faith in Christ is discouraged. If the leaders of a church share the love of Christ in all they say and do, witnessing is encouraged. When they fail to do this, witnessing is discouraged. And it's just like that. Sharing faith in Christ is not just something that is spoken, it is also a way of life. It is living in God's ways. Love God, love man, make disciples.

New Christians should feel especially supported as they share their faith. When someone accepts Jesus as their Lord and Savior and they are born again, they sense a wonderful change and can't keep quiet about this newness. They are compelled to tell people about what God is doing in their life. These new converts are on fire for God. This fire comes from Him into a surrendered heart! As they learn to love and obey Him, they learn to gradually surrender and are molded by Him as a potter molds the clay. This molding produces constant change and newness. They have power in their life to witness to others about this wonderful filling of God. I've seen church after church after church, subtly stifle this witness and miss opportunities to encourage and train their flock. The church doesn't grow, and the battle is lost, as the church is ineffective in the Great Commission.

When you encourage someone to witness by example, teach them the Biblical foundation of the salvation story, and verbally encourage them to use their gifts to work with other church members to go and love, your church will become a Smiling Church. God is working and using you to do His work. You have Power in your church.

Let's take a look at the last words Jesus spoke on earth. Acts 1:8 states, "But you shall receive power when the Holy Spirit has come upon you; and you shall be my witness in Jerusalem and in all Judea and Samar'ia and to the end of the earth." Make no mistake about it! A witness can come only from God! The Holy Spirit will glorify the Lamb. John 16:14 reads, "He will glorify Me."

Only God can draw men unto Himself to be saved. Only God can cause a church to grow and multiply from new converts. Only God can cause believers to grow in faith. Hebrews 12:2 states, "looking to Jesus the pioneer and perfecter of our faith." The direct translation from the original Greek here is "leader and completer."

I have talked and worked with scores of pastors and probably thousands of other church leaders and church people. In churches that are effective brides of Christ in the Great Commission, I hear and see a witness (people sharing their faith and events linked to God) that flows like a river. In churches that are not effective, I hear religious talk about one's involvement in religion. The difference is as great as day and night. Please note: If you read John Wesley's diaries, you will find that he described many conversations and labeled them 'religious talk.' What he was referring to was talk that described God's involvement in everyday life as one walked in His ways. The religious talk that I have referred to above in this paragraph is quite different as it describes talk about one's involvement in religion.

Now back to Acts. Please don't brush over the second chapter of Acts. The first verse tells us of the unity the disciples experienced with each other [and the women—Acts 1:14].

They had just enjoyed forty days of radiant appearances (Acts 1:3) with the risen Jesus as He taught them about the Kingdom of God. We can assume that this was in preparation for them to start the Great Commission, and also provided absolute proof of His Resurrection. The period between His ascension and Pentecost was ten days.

Acts 2:2-4 states, "And suddenly a sound came from heaven like the rush of a mighty wind, and it filled all the house where they were sitting. And there appeared tongues as of fire, distributed and resting on each one of them. And they were all filled with the Holy Spirit and began to speak in other tongues, as the Spirit gave them utterance." People from many other countries who spoke different languages were there and were amazed to hear the apostles speak in their own language. You must read verses five through thirteen to understand the effect it had on everyone in attendance.

In Acts 2:17-21, Peter quoted the prophet Joel and told of God's outpouring of the Holy Spirit on mankind, to those who have been chosen. Our intended service to God is described in verses thirty-eight and thirty-nine as a repented life **filled** with the Holy Spirit, a gift to those who He calls. We are talking about a deliverance from the spiritual dimension of fallen man, and a new birth into a life in a dimension one cannot know exists without the filling. There is no formula for doing this. You simply must recognize and confess your prideful will and sinful ways. You must have a heart to be a surrendered follower of Christ, and turn from your sins. On that glorious day, Peter preached the first born again message of the Great Commission and three thousand souls entered the Kingdom of God. If this isn't exciting I don't know what is.

Love. Do newcomers feel comfortable when visiting your church? Picture yourself in the car with them as they approach your church for the very first time. Does your parking lot have easy-to-find, first-time visitor spaces? Is the parking lot staff helpful and friendly? Walk in the door with them. Are greeters smiling and genuinely delighted that they have come? We are reaching out to souls with many different financial and social situations. Are some of your greeters in casual clothes? It is very important to have a portion of your greeters that are casually dressed.

Does each visitor receive a visitor's packet? Take a look around. What do you see? Are ushers waiting to show them around and guide them to a seat? Are the seats comfortable? Is the lighting soft in the seating area, just enough to read the Bible, and brighter on stage? Are people that are seated around them happy they are there? Listen. Is the sound adjusted to exactly the right volume? Is the worship team transparent but leading the music so that one voice is lifted to God in love? Is this church experience better than any movie or TV show, because you know beyond any shadow of doubt that your Creator is amongst you? Does the announcer talk about activities and small groups and describe how easy it is to get involved? Does the pastor relate the content of his or her message to what is happening in their own life?

Similarly, when a newcomer visits a small group, do they feel like family?

John 15:5. Everyone involved in planning and running the service must abide in Him. This includes the pastor and pastoral prayer team, ushers, parking lot staff, greeters, and worship team. Strength and direction must come from Him, for apart from Him, we can do nothing (good).

My calling is to help any Bible-believing church that wants to change into a "Smiling Church," and redirect their energy, their prayer, their time, their habits, and their hearts. Without Jesus at the helm, 'Nothing' will be redirected properly.

In my new home church the leaders do not differentiate between sins. They **love** everybody. We all have hidden scrolls, but those who are saved are justified through faith in Jesus. Through their example we are taught to love, and invite all to accept Christ. These leaders have no façade of self-righteousness. Please read chapters one through eight of Romans, and read the third chapter at least twice.

Joining home groups, journaling groups, and outreaches are all strongly encouraged in my new church. Each leader belongs to a journaling group, a home group, and advises in the organization of outreaches. New members are offered help to discover their own spiritual gifts and calling. When you listen to a sermon you hear a witness. When you are in a hallway, and catch what a leader says to a newcomer, you hear a witness. You hear a witness in the small groups, in the journaling groups, and the outreaches. When you hang around one of these leaders, you sense the motivation of Jesus in their speech and see it in their actions. You are taught by example. These leaders are filled with the Holy Spirit and are on fire for God!

Trust is a building block in the character of a Christian, and in the character of a church. The very act of trusting your time to Him as you budget time for Bible reading, ministering in your job, and attending a home group speaks volumes about you. Learning His ways by reading His word will teach you about trust, but actually walking in His ways and committing your time, money, energy, and life's being to Him will strengthen your trust. Speaking of money... all of the Smiling Churches that I have attended have had a high percentage of members that tithe, and also commit extra money to the poor. I have noticed that my new home church has a council that decides what happens to church money. They allocate approximately three times the percentage you will find that most churches allocate for donating to others.

It must be clearly stated that neither man nor woman can think they can start a ministry and expect God to help them. It doesn't work like that. God is always working and we have to learn to recognize where and how so we can join Him in His work with surrendered hearts and hands. Only God can teach us how to do that. We must learn to listen to Him for our instructions. Only God can teach us how. John 10:27 states, "My sheep listen to my voice; I know them, and they follow me." See Matthew 10:32, Mark 16:15-16, Luke 9:1-2, John 15:16, and 1st Samuel 25:28

The War—And its Spiritual Battles

Here on planet earth, Satan is the ruler of the kingdom of the air. In Ephesians 2:2, the Bible describes him as, "the prince of the power of the air, the **spirit** that is now at work in the sons of disobedience." (emphasis added) The targets of the devil's deception are your relationships with God, your fellow man, and yourself. See Ephesians 2:1-3, Genesis 3:1-4, and Romans 7:14-25.

Satan is in the business of devouring souls. He tempts and deceives. He is crafty and causes confusion and presses your fear, pride, and anger buttons. He knows your weaknesses better than you do, and will come upon you with temptation and deception so as to cause you failure in your journey. Destroying your mind-set is his goal. He is the enemy of your soul. If you are not walking daily with Christ, he's got you. Read 1st Peter 5:8, Matthew 4:1-3, and Revelation 12:9.

The **only** way to walk with Christ is to be born again. John 3:3 states, " 'Truly, truly, I say to you, unless one is born anew, he cannot see the Kingdom of God.' " Please note that Jesus is the only path into the Kingdom. He is the Way. You must accept Him as your personal Lord and Savior with a totally surrendered heart.

The term 'born again' was commonly used in the Jewish world before Jesus used it, according to Wesley in his sermon number forty-five. When an adult heathen was converted to become a Jew, he was first baptized and then circumcised. When he was baptized he was said to be born again into the Jewish religion.

Jesus used the term in a stronger sense stating that to enter into the Kingdom of God you must be born of water and the Spirit. When a child is born, the child begins a new life outside the womb. I have witnessed hundreds and hundreds of people being 'born again' in the past twenty-nine years. These souls are filled with the Spirit of Jesus, and the Holy Spirit. They start changing right away. They are new creatures in Christ. My hope is that you would personally experience the exhilaration that **only** comes from God when you see a soul accept Jesus into their heart. Leading souls to Jesus is how we are commanded to fight the battle and win the war.

Whooops

About 12 years ago, a woman shook her finger in my face and said, "I grew up in this town and went to church every Sunday at the (deleted) Church, and not once did the minister say anything about being born again. This stuff that you talk about is a bunch of nonsense."

And More

A couple of years ago, I was invited to a birthday party where I knew very few people, except the guest of honor. When I walked in, there were obviously several different families represented, each clustered together and spaced around the room.

One family was gathered in a semicircle around a woman who appeared to be the matriarch of the family. I edged closer to hear what she was saying. It went like this: "The trouble with the world today is those born-agains. They screw up everything!"

You Heard it, Too?

When I was a teenager and just entering my wild stage, I went to an old man for mentoring and advice. The old man taught me not to trust anyone and to "Stay away from the do-gooders and the born-agains. Those people don't know how to mind their own business." He also taught me how to drink whiskey.

Misconception

In my opinion, there is a misconception going around about self. In the long run, bragging about self or 'he or she who dies with the most toys wins,' won't bring eternal joy. Committing a balanced portion of your time, energy, money, and self to serving God in the job He chose for you will get you the peace you long for. All of a sudden, one day, you will realize that His love for you is something you can feel from the inside, and your walk with Him is eternal. John 14:20 states, "In that day you will know that I am in My Father, and you in me and I in you." And John 14:27 states, "Peace I leave with you; my peace I give to you; not as the world gives do I give to you. Let not your hearts be troubled, neither let them be afraid." See 2nd Corinthians 4:16-17 and 1st John 4:8.

The Truth

In addition to the benefit of eternal fire insurance, being born again will assure you of a connection and love affair with Almighty God that will last forever. You can't learn to walk in all of His ways and be sanctified without being born again. You also can't experience the deep peace of Jesus, or the most valuable thing a person can possess while living on this earth...the peace of mind that comes from God when you are serving Him in your chosen work. Only when you are born anew will you receive the Holy Spirit and Jesus will be in your heart and in your mouth.

Without being born again, you cannot begin to understand your role in the Great Commission. You also can't engage effectively in spiritual battles using the full armor that the Lord supplies in the Power of His might, or deal with the fiery darts of the enemy.

The devil will do his best to keep you separated from God by sin and render you useless in this "War for Souls." Second Corinthians 10:3-4 states, "For though we live in the world we are not carrying on a worldly war, for the weapons of our warfare are not worldly but have divine power to destroy strongholds." See also: John 10:25-30, John 14:25-27, Ephesians 1:3-11, Acts 26:9-18, Matthew 28:16-20, Romans 8:18-30, John 10:10, Romans 5:1, Isaiah 59:2, and John 14:15-17.

You Decide

To break the devil's worldly cycle and enter into God's cycle of love and eternal life with Him, you must confess that you are a sinner, repent, and accept Christ Jesus as your personal Savior and Lord, and surrender your heart to Him. John 10:27-28 states, "My sheep hear my voice, and I know them, and they follow me; and I give them eternal life, and they shall never perish, and no one is able to snatch them out of the Father's hand." John 14:5-6 states, "Thomas said to Him, 'Lord, we do not know where you are going; how can we know the way?' Jesus said to him, 'I Am the Way, and the Truth, and the Life; no one comes to the Father but by Me.' "

God loves us so much that He sacrificed His Son, the only Righteous One, for us on the Cross, so that if we accept Jesus as our Lord and Savior we can be saved. Being saved means we are forgiven of our sins so we are no longer separated from God, and will be saved from the wrath of God which leads to the second death on judgment day. Being saved also means that we are saved by His grace, receiving not the death we deserve, but eternal life; and that we are saved for the purpose that He created us for.

When you are then saved, my Savior will give you a different perspective. James 4:7 commands, "Submit yourselves therefore to God. Resist the devil and he will flee from you. Draw near to God and He will draw near to you." James 4:10 reads, "Humble yourselves before the Lord and He will exalt you." See Romans 3:23, Romans 10:9, John 3, Mark 1:14-15, and 1st Peter 3:18.

God's plan for each of us is to have a close, personal relationship with Him that grows and lasts forever. He is Love and He is Holy. He created all of us for His pleasure. When you accept Christ as your Lord and Savior you begin a love affair that will never end. Being born again means that you are being delivered from the one-dimensional spiritual world that the devil controls, because of the fall of man. It means that you are being joined to God as you accept His ways, surrender your heart and soul and will to Him, turn from your sinful ways (repent), and live forever with Him in agreement. Your soul and spirit and body are then connected with God.

Being born again is a birthing process made possible by the blood that Christ sacrificed for you on the Cross—in atonement for your sins. As you confess that you are a sinner and accept Christ as your Lord and Savior, the blood that Jesus shed for you is so powerful that you are cleansed, you are forgiven. When you truly lift up your heart, soul, and will to Him in surrender forever, the birthing is complete and in a moment you become a child of God—and He becomes your Father.

Only when you are born again will He reveal the depth and awe of His holiness. You cannot possibly understand His glory, splendor, love, and power, or be able to hear His voice without the indwelling Spirit that He has reserved for those who will truly surrender their heart and will to Him. In order to walk in His ways you have to be in agreement with Him. Scholars throughout the centuries have read the Bible and scoffed at its principles and examples. Only when you are born again will the true meaning of the Word be revealed to you. It is special and of a dimensional, spiritual world that no one can perceive without being filled with God's Spirit.

Our wonderful Heavenly Father is much more intelligent than the human mind can conceive. God's thoughts are of a much higher nature than ours. He created all that is created. We can't do that or even imagine how. Isaiah 55:8-9 shows us the truth, "For my thoughts are not your thoughts, neither are your ways my ways, says the Lord. For the heavens are higher than the earth, so are my ways higher than your ways and my thoughts than your thoughts."

God is Holy. He made the rules and will enforce them. Because He is Holy, **all** sin is dealt with. Rebellious souls have long bolstered each other in their pride to overthrow [in their own spirits] His righteousness.

God is positive. The devil is the source of negativity. The evil one will constantly urge you to be negative toward reverence to God's rules and His righteousness. You may be compelled to join others in order to spoil or put down a Christian's righteous project. The one-dimensional spirit world you are trapped in won't let you see it any other way. Only Jesus can rescue you from this and bring the Truth into your soul.

Look to God's Word as the richest source of Truth. The discipline of doing what is holy will gain you pleasures more sustaining than short-term, worldly pleasures. The peaceful fruit of righteousness is sweet and lasting. The lure of irreverent behavior promises to feel good now, and gives a feeling of **power**. That feeling of power is very addictive, but will inevitably lead to misery and sorrow later.

Like Wesley, I was an Almost Christian for years. I went to churches faithfully, listened to sermons, was involved in church activities, and even talked privately with ministers about theology. Now I know that there is a night and day difference when you are born anew in your spirit, and accept Jesus and all of God's ways. You then possess a love for God that fills the whole heart, and you can understand why James (in the second chapter of James) wrote about one's motivation to obey and serve.

You can prove the Truth of my statements. Cast aside your pride and negativity and ask God. Just saying the words is not enough. You must earnestly seek Him from your heart. Even if you have never heard about any of this before, ask God if these statements are true.

Do it even if you believe in God but feel that He is distant. Even if you have attended a Christian church every Sunday your whole life, and never heard that you must be born again, please ask Him. You may already be part of a Christian ministry and think this theology of mine is all wet. Nonetheless, if you have never heard His voice or possessed the deep peace of Jesus, give yourself this chance to lay your soul completely before Him. Talk to Him with this prayer:

> Dear God, this book has challenged me to see if you are really there and to question the validity of being born a second time, a new birth of my soul, spirit, and body that has been held captive in the one-dimensional spirit world of the fall of man. I am now humbling myself and asking, "Are you real?" If You truly are, I want to tap that mighty vein of Power this book talks about. At this very moment, I agree to humble myself, give up my pride, turn over my heart and soul to You, and accept Your Son Jesus as my personal Lord and Savior. I confess that I am a sinner. Let it happen that I will be drawn to Jesus, repent, and be saved. Amen.

Hearing about salvation usually comes from a one-on-one talk, and includes a testimony of faith. All Christian churches should encourage sharing the message of salvation, while remembering that the enemy in this War is subtle and wise. A church can easily fall into one of Satan's well-laid traps. In my own private thinking I call the most common the 'Us versus Them' trap. Let me explain. Living with the knowledge of the two different spiritual worlds is sometimes frustrating because you want to tell people what they are missing but the enemy of their soul makes it impossible for them to understand. Also, as you learn to love God you get upset at the constant rejection of His righteousness. If you are not careful the devil will tempt you with anger, and you will start pointing fingers, and be tempted to openly condemn people for their irreverent behavior and rebellious assaults on God. Then you create an "Us against Them" mind-set. The world stops seeing love and can only interpret your actions as hate.

Serving the Lord should be fun and is always very rewarding.

Living in the cycle of joy, peace, and love comes with a satisfaction that stems from the indwelling of Jesus. Falling into an enemy trap can stop the fun.

Twenty-nine years of being on the road has taught me that there is only one reason why a person won't humble him or herself and surrender their soul to Almighty God. That reason is pride, which is one of the devil's greatest weapons in his arsenal that he uses to separate us from the Truth. Other weapons include lust, negativity towards God's righteousness, and fear of what your peers will think. Satan tempts and accuses. History shows us that Satan's influence has directed many brilliant minds to reject being born again. Psalm 81:12 states, "So I gave them over to their stubborn hearts to follow their own counsels."

The deck is stacked. People who are highly intelligent, or possess above average good looks, or are extremely talented (especially in the arts) face odds that are very much against them. It is sport for their enemy to master and manipulate them to elevate themselves and prevent them from seeking God. Only a few of these poor souls seem able to break the enemy's strong control. It is impossible for even the brightest people in the world to understand the Bible without the Holy Spirit's guidance. Human reasoning in its highest form fails to comprehend that the Truth is a person.

Let's read the richness of Truth in 1st Corinthians 1:17-25 which tells us, "For Christ did not send me to baptize but to preach the gospel, and not with eloquent wisdom, lest the cross of Christ be emptied of its power.

For the word of the cross is folly to those who are perishing, but to us who are being saved it is the power of God. For it is written,

'I will destroy the wisdom of the wise, and the

cleverness of the clever I will thwart.'

Where is the wise man? Where is the scribe? Where is the debater of this age? Has not God made foolish the wisdom of the world? For since, in the wisdom of God, the world did not know God through wisdom, it pleased God through the folly of what we preach to save those who believe. For Jews demand signs and Greeks seek wisdom, but we preach Christ crucified, a stumbling-block to Jews and folly to Gentiles, but to those who are called, both Jews and Greeks, Christ the power of God and the wisdom of God. For the foolishness of God is wiser than men, and the weakness of God is stronger than men."

A few years back I was at a convention with a friend. During each block of time we had to choose whether to stay in the main auditorium and listen to a speaker, or attend one of the workshops in smaller rooms down the corridors. We decided to sit for a while, relax, and listen to the next speaker. The man left his seat in the front row to make his way up to the stage and while doing so was introduced as 'the most intelligent Christian on earth.' For the first two or three minutes, my friend and I were still whispering about the last workshop. All of a sudden something strange happened. Each of us, and I'm sure the other several thousand that were in the room came to a place of complete attention in our focus on this man's statements. It was almost like we were receiving his thoughts from a wave of direct current that we were plugged into.

The man speaking was humble and works in orphanages in war-torn countries. He simply talked about the love of the God we serve, and how we are to love as Christ directs. He also talked about God's character in us versus the character of Satan in the worldly. He explained the difference between a Christian's walk and a worldly person's nature. Mind you, this was a long time ago. I didn't get his name and took no notes, but still remember the gist of what he said. Lust [of the flesh and of the eye] and pride [giving glory to self] motivate the worldly. Loving people and giving glory to God motivate one who is born again. Lust desires to get while love desires to give. Lust serves self but love serves others. Lust wants to benefit self at the expense of others while love wants to benefit others at the expense of self. If you would like to study these differences more deeply I suggest reading "The Potential Principle" by Edwin Louis Cole.

Pride is reserved for family. A parent is proud of their child's accomplishments. Do your actions and speech make your heavenly Father proud of you?

Serving your Father breaks through the negativity of the devil and opens more of God's positive, spiritual world to you; so each phase of your walk with God brings satisfaction and joy. He won't take you out of the troubles and strife of this world but will give you grace to live in it. John 17:13-19 says, "But now I am coming to thee; and these things I speak in the world, that they may have my joy fulfilled in themselves. I have given them thy word; and the world has hated them because they are not of the world, even as I am not of the world. I do not pray that thou shouldst take them out of the world, but that thou shouldst keep them from the evil one. They are not of the world, even as I am not of the world. Sanctify them in the truth; thy word is truth. As thou didst send me into the world, so I have sent them into the world. And for their sake I consecrate myself, that they also may be consecrated in truth."

Helping others in obedience to God gives you His joy and His strength. This joy lives within you and empowers you to serve. A dynamic starts happening as your relationship with God grows. Your faith starts bringing expectation, which leads to success and strengthens your faith. Knowing He is pleased with your character growth and work leads to an even deeper sense of joy. He will also give you a growing compassion for serving mankind.

He wants us to walk with Him in peace through all situations. Please realize that Jesus is there with you through the storms and will be there to restore your spirit when you are ready. There is a misconception that God sometimes wants us to be miserable. Wrong, that's the goal of the devil.

Two thousand years ago Jesus prayed for you and those that you lead to Him as you go and love. John 17:20-21 gives us this knowledge, "I do not pray for these only, but also those who are to believe in me through their word, that they may all be one; even as thou Father, art in me, and I in thee, that they also may be in us, so that the world may believe that thou hast sent me."

Victory in Jesus causes one to smile.

Nehemiah 8:10 says, "for the joy of the Lord is your strength." Also, consider John 15:11, which shows us the positive effect of His indwelling love, "These things I have spoken to you, that my joy may be in you, and that your joy may be full."

Transformation

God will transform you. Your transformation (sanctification) is a wonderful, lifelong experience that progresses as you learn to surrender your own will to Him and trust Him in every area of your life. He will give you strength, wisdom, and guidance, and teach you His ways. The more you **learn** to surrender, the more He can mold you into the vessel He desires to do His work.

Your new life will go on forever [here and then in heaven] in fellowship with Him. This is all about becoming like Christ, the One who suffered and died in atonement for your sins on the Cross. Look at how the Truth is so beautifully woven through the Bible.

First, let's read John 1:1, which states, "In the beginning was the Word, and the Word was with God. He was in the beginning with God; all things were made through him, and without him was not anything made that was made. In him was life, and the life was the light of men. The light shines in the darkness, and the darkness has not overcome it."

Now we'll go to Genesis 1:26, which reads, "Then God said, 'Let us make man in our image, after our likeness;' " It's time to get the full picture of how these passages coincide with His purpose for us so we can completely understand the transformation process. These facts are stated in Romans 8:28-30, which says, "We know that in everything God works for good with those who love him, who are called according to his purpose. For those whom he foreknew he also predestined to be conformed to the image of his Son, in order that he might be the first-born among many brethren. And those whom he predestined he also called; and those whom he called he also justified; and those whom he justified he also glorified."

Finally let's read 2nd Corinthians 3:12-18, which tells us how exciting this process really is: "Since we have such a hope, we are very bold, not like Moses, who put a veil over his face so that the Israelites might not see the end of the fading splendor. But their minds were hardened; for to this day, when they read the old covenant, that same veil remains unlifted, because only through Christ is it taken away. Yes, to this day whenever Moses is read a veil lies over their minds; but when a man turns to the Lord the veil is removed. Now the Lord is the Spirit, and where the Spirit of the Lord is, there is freedom. And we all, with unveiled face, beholding the glory of the Lord, are being changed into his likeness from one degree of glory to another; for this comes from the lord who is the Spirit."

Also see: Proverbs 3 and 30, Psalms 2, 4, 5, 7, 9, 11, 16, 17, 18, 20, 22, 25, 31, 34, 36, 37, 40, 52, 55, 61, 62, 64, 71, 73, 91, 115, 118, and 119; John 14:15-17; and Philippians 2:13.

Prayer

God is sovereign. He has created all that is created. He alone is in charge of the universe and all that there is.

Because of the fall of man we have to deal with constant evil and strife. After you have been born anew, you have the privilege of approaching the Master's throne of grace. Jesus is our intercessor. We can use His name when we humbly come to the Father. John 15:16 states, "You did not choose me, but I chose you and appointed you that you should go and bear fruit and that your fruit should abide; so that whatever you ask the Father in my name, he may give it to you." Please read John 14 and John 16:23-28 to gain a better understanding.

I have been taught that there are three parts to prayer: confession, praise, and supplication.

Confession: As old things pass away, and we become a new creature in Christ, we learn more about how to examine ourselves, and how and what to confess. Confession of sin with an attitude of repentance and surrendering your will to Him is needed. Ask God for forgiveness and make sure you learn to forgive others. If at first it's hard to do, ask for help. Please read Mark 11:20-26.

Praise: Reflect on His greatness, and all He has done for you when you praise Him. We humans don't have the capacity to fully understand His power and His love, but as your relationship with Him grows, you will get a glimpse. Your faith and trust in Him will increase and become a big part of your life. Luke 11:2 states, "And he said to them, 'When you pray, say, Father, hallowed be thy name.'"

Supplication: Lay your burdens down and those of others. He loves to hear from your heart. Please read the sixth chapter of Matthew. See Luke 11:1-13, Galatians 3:22, Galatians 1:3-5, Psalm 51, Psalm 7:17, Psalm 66, Deuteronomy 4:7, 1st John 5:14, John 14:10-14, Philippians 1:3-6, 1st Samuel 1:9-17, 1st Samuel 1:19-20, and 1st Samuel 2:1-10.

My brother-in-law, Doug, recently sent me an e-mail that talked about people who research happiness. They recommend trying a new exercise. Each night think about three good things that happened that day and analyze why they happened. Through time you are to expand this thinking. Over the past twenty-nine years, I have stopped at least three times a day to thank the Lord for the many blessings He has caused to happen. As I talk to Him I go over each one in detail. No wonder I experience joy.

I also would like to bring up the fact that I have experienced sorrow intermittently in my life. It is my opinion that developing an understanding of God's restoration and healing helps us think positively about the future. Living in Christ will keep you focused on a servant's journey on earth, a journey of satisfaction. God is very concerned that we learn to live a holy life, and be content in Christ in all circumstances. I firmly believe that serving God and man is infinitely more fulfilling than serving self. You have to take care of yourself and your family, but learning a balance, and reflecting on the positive and joyous times is the key to happiness.

Jesus came to love, heal, and forgive; and to reveal the Kingdom of God. He also enriches our lives with His joy that dwells within us after we are born anew and are being sanctified. Kathryn Kuhlman used to laugh, and yell out, "You are rich! Peace of mind is the most valuable thing that man can possess! Only God can give you that!" We all know that life on earth is a dual existence. There are always joys and there are always problems. The most important thing you can do for yourself is to grow in spiritual character as you gradually achieve Christ likeness in your sanctification, and remember the private times that He was in deep prayer with His Father. It is only Jesus who can give you the peace that Kathryn talked about. Seek a closer walk with your Savior.

When you properly fear, respect, and trust Almighty God in your heart it is easier to pray; and don't forget—the One who died for you is always there to help.

1st Peter 4:7-11 states, "The end of all things is at hand; therefore keep sane and sober for your prayers. Above all hold unfailing your love for one another, since love covers a multitude of sins. Practice hospitality ungrudgingly to one another. As each has received a gift, employ it for one another, as good stewards of God's varied grace: whoever speaks, as one who utters oracles of God; whoever renders service, as one who renders it by the strength which God supplies; in order that in everything God may be glorified through Jesus Christ. To him belong glory and dominion for ever and ever. Amen."

Luke 11:1-4 in the original Greek says, "And it came to pass as was he in a place certain praying, when he ceased, said one of his disciples to him, Lord, teach us to pray, as also John taught his disciples. And he said to them, 'When ye pray say, Father our, who [art] in the heavens, sanctified be thy name; let come thy Kingdom; let be done thy will, as in heaven, [so] also upon earth. Our bread the needed give us daily; and forgive us our sins, for also ourselves we forgive every one indebted to us; and lead not us into temptation, but deliver us from evil.' "

Reasons for Smiling

When you are sanctified you are set apart for God's purpose and are continually being made in Christ's image. This is more exciting than you can imagine. Your daily reading of the Bible will also, gradually, become surprisingly exciting when you first ask the Holy Spirit to guide you.

When you are truly born again and surrender your heart to Him you are justified which means He declares you righteous and blameless. Jesus died to pay the penalty for your sin. When you accept Jesus by faith and put your trust in Him, God declares you not guilty. You become righteous because only Jesus lived a life of perfect righteousness, which in turn is imputed to you. This righteousness comes only from God. Man cannot attain this righteousness on his own. Being justified also means to be 'proved' to be free from the penalty of sin. Don't be confused. This does not come about as the end result of a lifetime of struggling to rid yourself of sin to achieve salvation, but rather you are justified, right now, with God's stamp of approval, by faith alone.

As you gain a deeper understanding of this gift of salvation, the freedom is overwhelmingly wonderful. The love back and forth between you and your Savior will cause you to smile. Pleasing Him becomes the highest priority. Romans 3:21-26 states, "But now the righteousness of God has been manifested apart from law, although the law and the prophets bear witness to it, the righteousness of God through faith in Jesus Christ for all who believe. For there is no distinction; since all have sinned and fall short of the glory of God, they are justified by his grace as a gift, through the redemption which is in Christ Jesus, whom God put forward as an expiation by His blood, to be received by faith. This was to show God's righteousness, because in His divine forbearance He had passed over former sins; it was to prove at the present time that He Himself is righteous and that He justifies him who has faith in Jesus."

We should understand, in the text above, the significance of the Power of Christ's blood. In 1899 Lewis E. Jones wrote the beautiful old Hymn, "There is Power in the Blood." He put a pleasant and now familiar melody to the Truth—there is wonder-working Power in the precious blood of the Lamb. 'Expiation,' or as some translations say 'propitiation,' means 'atoning sacrifice.' It is helpful here to study Leviticus 16:14 and the Old Testament look into the future event of Christ on the Cross. The blood that was sprinkled seven times before the mercy seat represents the perfection and completion of atonement that the sacrifice of our Savior would bring. Leviticus 16:14 tells us, "and he shall take some of the blood of the bull, and sprinkle it with his finger on the front of the mercy seat, and before the mercy seat he shall sprinkle the blood with his finger seven times."

Please read Leviticus 17:11.

May you be blessed with daily awareness that the defining event of the Bible centers around Christ on the Cross—the most important moment for mankind. The Power of the Cross gives a righteousness which is not our own, but of God, to those who believe.

These passages in Romans are so important also, because of Passover. Christian churches should equip all of Jesus' disciples with a total understanding of Passover and the blood of the Lamb. Please study the twelfth chapter of Exodus. God used His mighty right hand and was personally involved in the rescue of His people. The more you learn about every detail surrounding Passover and of history since that time, including your salvation, the more you will adore the heart of our Father. This study will draw you closer to Him.

You will find approximately eighty references to Passover in the Bible. It's all about Jesus. Did you ever see a bumper sticker that says, "Smile God loves you" and realize the sacrifice He paid for your soul? When your reciprocating heart pours out love back to Him your service will be carried by His strength, and you won't be able to stop telling people how wonderful He is.

1st Corinthians 5:7 says, "For Christ, our paschal lamb, has been sacrificed." Paschal means 'Lamb of God.'

God is Holy and cannot be in the presence of sin. When our Father looks into the undivided heart of a confessing sinner He sees the blood of His Son and is satisfied with the price that was paid for our atonement, thus we are found acceptable.

Romans 10:10-11 gives us a reason to smile now, on Judgment Day, and forever, "For a man believes with his heart and so is justified, and he confesses with his lips and so is saved. The scripture says, 'No one who believes in him will be put to shame.' "

See Romans 5 & 6, Isaiah 53, Acts 18:38-39, 1st John 5:10-12, and Galatians 3:3, 3:11-14.

An Apparent Contradiction

Many, many people start studying the Bible, and sooner or later, read James 2:24, which states, "You see that a man is justified by works and not by faith alone." They compare this verse with Paul's statements about being justified by faith alone, and dismiss it as a contradiction. **It is not.**

Throughout the New Testament there are several references to faith and belief in Jesus. Let's look at John 3:16, which tells us, "For God so loved the world that he gave his only Son, that whoever believes in him should not perish but have eternal life." James was making the point that you could get confused and think that you can be saved and not perish, and be justified by simply believing in Jesus. You cannot.

To be justified you must have a faith in your heart that comes only from indwelling love. This type of faith inwardly motivates a soul to do good works. Genuine faith cannot sit still. It must take action. We are talking about a faith that must obey God and serve Him. James gives examples of this genuine faith, so strong, that those who truly believe in Him, in their heart, will surrender all they are and have to do His work.

James 2:18-26 states, "But some will say, 'You have faith and I have works.' Show me your faith apart from your works, and I by my works will show you my faith. You believe that God is one; you do well. Even the demons believe...and shudder. Do you want to be shown, you foolish fellow, that faith apart from works is barren? Was not Abraham our father justified by works, when he offered his son Isaac upon the altar? You see that faith was active along with his works, and the scripture was fulfilled which says, 'Abraham believed God, and it was reckoned to him as righteousness'; and he was called the friend of God.

You see that a man is justified by works and not by faith alone. And in the same way was not also Rahab the harlot justified by works when she received the messengers and sent them out another way? For as the body apart from the spirit is dead, so faith apart from works is dead."

James distinguishes between having this genuine faith in Christ and merely acknowledging His existence. Demons believe in Jesus, and fully know that He created them; but they certainly wouldn't be motivated to work for Him. Nor are they justified. They serve the devil! They know that you can't serve two masters. James was talking in a different context about this complete definition of faith, which is based on a love from within that compels us to work. Anyone can believe in Jesus' existence, but without being connected to Him in love through this genuine, motivational faith, you cannot be justified.

Your Role

The Cycle of Joy, Peace, and Love is my name for an individual's role in the Great Commission. First you are drawn to Jesus and accept Him as your personal Lord and Savior. Then you join a Bible believing church, learn to serve God in your chosen purpose using the gifts that you were uniquely created with, and are part of a body that loves God, loves man, and makes disciples of Christ.

You will become a member of an ongoing outreach that shares God's love for mankind in a war to rescue fallen man from the bonds of the dimension that the devil controls—a war in which saved souls then enter the Cycle, are filled with the Holy Spirit, and help rescue others.

When a soul first accepts Christ there is a time period in which the evil one tries to steal back the soul and destroy a person's work. Always remember to focus on Jesus, not the devil. In John 15:4 the secret for life on this planet is revealed, "Abide in Me, and I in you."

It is important that church people stay close to a new convert when the transformation is beginning. I'll be grinning from ear-to-ear if you tell me it's standard practice in your church to give newly saved people a ride to church for a couple of weeks. It is also vitally important to get them into a disciple class for five to seven weeks, so they can get an overview of the Bible, be stimulated to read it every day, and start learning the character of our God.

As time goes on, the church should help new Christians identify their spiritual gifts and encourage them to use these gifts as they join the Lord in His work as part of a fellowship that reaches out to the lost and the poor, in the Cycle of Joy, Peace, and Love. Then the cycle is repeated as they actively work as part of a group that reaches out to the lost and leads more souls into the Cycle. This is the fulfillment of the Great Commission.

The topic of purpose keeps surfacing. Before God formed the foundations of the earth He knew you. He knew when He would physically create you, your skills, your personality, your likes and dislikes; Almighty God knew who you are to the smallest detail. You were created to accept Jesus as your personal Lord and Savior, and serve Him as a member of the body of Christ, and your purpose in the Cycle will glorify God.

Your Group of Love

What a wonderful feeling to serve the Lord as part of a home group (or you might call them small groups, home prayer groups, weekly fellowship groups, or cell groups, etc.), meeting once a week in harmony, usually in a member's home. Meetings open humbly with prayer and praise. Then, the pastor's weekly message **is reviewed and studied**. This brings unity to the church, helps each member grow in the wisdom and knowledge of God, and moves the church forward.

Reviewing the pastor's sermon in weekly home groups is an absolute requirement for achieving and maintaining unity in a church, yet very few churches do so. Not reviewing the pastor's sermon will result in nothing but problems as it is almost impossible for a flock of believers to move forward without this vital time utilized in home groups. There are exceptions, of course, but it has been my experience that this step helps create oneness.

The **next** major time allocation on the agenda is to discuss each person's involvement in outreach. Your church is unique, and your individual souls are unique. God will tailor ministries accordingly, to surrendered hearts. Outreach includes all functions within the church, and the love directed toward your community and other communities wherever they may be. Misunderstanding the coupling of the inside-church and outside-church efforts to achieve a common goal of going and loving will result in nothing but problems. It is almost impossible for a flock to move forward, and grow by multiplication, if the church isn't unified with this directed, concerted mind-set. All callings are equally important as they are linked together to love God, love man, and make disciples.

Next, **pray** for each household around the host home and each household around each member's home neighborhood. Pray that these souls would be drawn to Jesus as He stated in John 6:44 ("No one can come to me unless the Father who sent me draws him; and I will raise him up on the last day."), so as to be saved from God's wrath, and saved for God's purpose. Then, discuss and decide when and who will approach each household to invite them to your group, and to church.

Inform all newcomers about the price God paid for their souls. Explain the complete salvation message and invite them to accept Christ as their Lord and Savior.

Getting to know all these people will inevitably lead you to some that are poor, sick, hurting, and some that have a loved one in jail. Each needy person you meet represents an opportunity to minister in God's love. Reaching out in this way will impact your community and lead many new souls to Christ, and to your church. See Acts 1:8,

4:29, and 22:15.

The **fourth** and final item on the home group agenda is ending the meeting with heartfelt prayer. I suggest making a weekly list of your supplications and praises that you lift up to the Lord, and assign members to pray for requests on the list, and thank Him for the answered prayers.

After the structured part of the meeting is complete, enjoy each other's fellowship.

It is my firm belief that part of the richness of life can be felt and shared in a church home group. Close relationships form as you learn about and pray for each other. Even large churches can keep that small, comfortable feeling because of home groups. Home groups inevitably grow to overflowing and must multiply, but the friendships carry on.

There are many ways to grow a church and reach out to a community. In my experience, properly run home groups are the single most effective method I've seen and they cause a whole lot of people to smile. Also, these groups by their very nature seem to stop cliques from forming in a church. They also create sheep dogs, if you will, that can spot wolves who are circling the flock. See James 2:14-26, James 1:22, 1st John 1 & 2, Acts 20:25-31, and 1st John 4 ... God is love.

Before I write each page of this book I ask the Lord to give me every word, and I write about personal experiences and how they relate to wisdom He has given me. Some home groups carry on for years and years while others shut down for various reasons. I have not been given knowledge of all of the reasons why these things happen. There is an excellent book that discusses these issues as well most other details involved in starting and maintaining healthy small groups. I would highly recommend that you read, "House To House" by Larry Kreider.

Referring to John

In case you are wondering, when you see us gathered in the corner of the church foyer talking about Wesley, the man we are referring to is John Wesley (1703-1790).

John and his brother Charles, noted for the many hymns he wrote, were raised in a very strict religious family. Their great-grandfather was a minister, their grandfather was a minister, their father a rector, and their mother was a very powerful leader of large prayer meetings. John had aspirations to become a minister from a very early age. He received a Masters from Oxford and was ordained in the Anglican Church in 1728.

Wesley went to the American Colony of Georgia in 1735 for the purpose of converting American Indians to Christianity. All his life he believed that salvation was achieved largely through works, by being holy enough to satisfy God's standards, and pursuing a life-long rebirth in the likeness of Christ. At the time, he understood these works to be part of this process of salvation that comes in the struggle towards holiness.

On the ship to America he met and observed a group of German Moravians who were part of the Pietist movement, started in the 1670s by Phillip Jakob Spener, which influenced German Lutherans to be born again. Wesley became friends with one of these Germans, Peter Bohler. It was Peter Bohler years later, back in England, who led first Charles and then John to be saved. This came about because John was struck by the living faith of the Germans, and their lack of fear and doubt. He thoroughly studied their interpretation of the Bible, and Luther's commentary on Galatians. He then realized that, in Acts, God worked instantaneously. This faith that saves, this warm and personal relationship with Jesus, and the righteousness and joy in the Holy Spirit, could be given and received in a moment.

Back in England, in 1737, John went to Charles and had heated discussions. John's stance contradicted all they had been taught. Charles eventually agreed to meet with Peter Bohler. This meeting resulted in a long conversation. It was May 21, 1738 when it pleased God to open Charles' eyes. It was then that Charles was born again. Two days later Charles Wesley started writing hymns. He wanted the world to know about this grace of God, this free gift of salvation that happens in a moment, bought for him and everyone else by Jesus' sacrifice on the cross.

It has been recorded that John started teaching 'you must be born again' to a condemned prisoner two months before this. On March 6, 1738 John offered this man salvation by faith in Christ alone. The man accepted Jesus into his heart, was born again, and walked to his death filled with peace.

On May 24, 1738 John Wesley went to a Moravian society meeting off Aldersgate Street in London. He accepted Jesus fully into his heart and felt the warm, personal experience that one sometimes does when filled with the Holy Spirit. He was born again.

He spent the rest of his life trying to set the record straight, explaining that the assurance of salvation was through trust in Christ alone. Sins are taken away and one is saved in a moment from the law of sin and death. Wesley preached, wrote, and constantly traveled, mostly by horseback, (or as he called whatever his current horse happened to be) his mount, for fifty-two more years.

Lucky for us, Wesley felt a personal need to record almost all he thought about or said or did. There are many experts when it comes to the knowledge of Wesley's life. I certainly am not one of them, but have intermittently read his diaries, and also a couple of biographies about him. He was very human, sometimes contrapuntal, but always preoccupied with doing the best he could to serve his Creator. He worked very hard and had the mind-set that we should suffer for

Christ, thus he constantly fasted and denied himself pleasures. When it came to money, he believed in giving and giving and giving.

Wesley blatantly talked about the Almost Christian. He said that the Almost Christian's purpose is to get sinners to accept the forgiveness that is in Jesus. He attempts to lead those who are seeking God into an understanding of Jesus. He attends church constantly, and avoids all improper actions and appearances while there. He has a form of godliness, does not return evil for evil, does not wittingly do wrong, strives to help those in need, strives to live in peace, abstains from drunkenness, and is sincere in his religion. He has a real and healthy desire to serve God and to do His will.

Wesley would go on and on about the Almost Christian saying that his knowledge came from personal experience because for many years he was an Almost Christian. He then compared the Almost Christian with the Altogether Christian, distinguished by being born again and described as having a love of God that fills the whole heart, without fear or doubt. The Altogether Christian has a love stronger than death, for both God and mankind. This divine love does the works of God, not man. John Wesley very seriously preached and wrote that this new birth is absolutely necessary to receive eternal salvation. You must be born again.

For several years Wesley would be told not to come back by many of the churches to whom he preached. This kind of preaching was too radical for many of the religious people of that day to tolerate.

By the end of his life things had turned around and he was heralded as a worthy teacher of the ways of God. John Wesley is considered to be the spiritual father of more than thirty-five denominations and movements. It is estimated that he traveled over a quarter of a million miles on horseback doing the work of his Father.

Wesley was humble and transparent, and was given an authority from God to speak. His witness was woven through all that he did like a golden thread. For this reason, I was compelled to write about him. His sermons on the Holy Spirit are fascinating treasures that I encourage all to read.

When I first started being a helper in the Great Commission, I got into several arguments with ministers in some of the very same denominations that Wesley inspired. They didn't want me talking to their congregation about this radical theology of being born again. How sad that, in some circles, the core of Wesley's message has been lost. Near the end of Wesley's life he occasionally expressed an apparent ambivalence about some of his earlier theological stances. It is my personal opinion that he never changed his conviction about one's heart being committed to Christ.

I don't argue anymore. I invite them, in His love, to read Wesley.

Back to the Mystery

Each one of us has his or her private thought language that we use in our reasoning process. Some-times this language includes words that we are reluctant (and maybe a little embarrassed) to share with others. For instance: I used the term "Smiling Church" privately for a long time before vocalizing it to anyone.

I have never told anyone, but I personally think of pastors and leaders of "Smiling Churches" as "HLs" because to me they represent Humble Love. While they are on this earth they are fully aware that they are shepherds in training, always leaning on Jesus for everything as they do the Father's work. These people seem to share a common thread that links them together. They are transparent and humble, and encourage the freedom that is found in walking with their Master who they love and adore. The hidden, joyful undercurrent found in their churches comes down to the same basic set of objectives: love God, love man, make disciples. Though they possess all the shortcomings of being human, they are preoccupied with learning about and talking to Jesus, and teaching others how to listen to and love Him.

During the initial years of my training, before He started revealing the solution, God had me constantly visiting many churches. I would try to enter unnoticed and slip into a seat to watch and listen. As well as working with a home church and helping others with outreaches, visiting different churches became a long-standing habit.

Sometimes a speaker will come out with words, in the context of their message, that are profoundly simple yet communicate their thoughts and personal, unique understanding of the topic.

One Sunday I was sitting in the back of a "Smiling Church" looking around and listening, and was fascinated by how much the congregation was swept away by this undercurrent of **love that flowed** around the room. The speaker was Pastor Lisa Bonanno. I turned my attention back to her to focus on what she was saying. Just then she said, "Jesus was always thinking about the harvest."

I would like to interject that our Lord drew me back to this particular church weeks later, and it has become my family's home church.

It has been my experience that this same flowing love spills out of the sanctuary into all that is going on in the church. From the welcoming hands of the greeters, to the smiles, friendliness, and handshakes of other church members, it is evident that these extended hands are connected to the heart. People can always sense sincerity when they are truly welcome, and feel comfortable in returning to future services.

Many of the churches I visited were just the opposite. They made me feel uncomfortable. It took years to figure out why. Other churches felt sort of comfortable, but something was missing. I went to a lot of them several times.

Here it is. I think a church's forward motion is slowed or stopped, rendering it unable to effectively win souls for Christ, when **spiritual battles** are unnoticed or are incorrectly identified. The enemy comes in and starts pushing pride and fear buttons and many battles are lost without a fight. In other words, the mission of the church gradually gets clouded by too much human understanding, priorities get shifted, and little problems get blown out of proportion. After a while, the focus is inward instead of outward and the horizontal priorities of man replace the vertical priorities of God. Without realizing it, the leaders ignore the Power of the Cross.

I now believe that changing most of these churches into "Smiling Churches" is much, much easier than you can possibly imagine. You see, our Father uses surrendered vessels for His work as His Kingdom comes to earth in the hearts of men. Our precious Lord Jesus is in charge of the harvest. He has all authority and goes to where our Father is working.

Changing a church starts in the hearts of the leadership. Total, humble surrender is the key. The pastor has to have a witness from God that echoes through his weekly message, his meetings, and his thinking. A prayer team should be formed for the sole purpose of praying for the pastor.

All leaders must have a witness that permeates their thoughts, speech, planning, and activities. Daily Bible reading for all leaders is vital. Through constant prayer of seeking His will, and guidance, the leadership has to gradually come about into one mind, realizing that Jesus' purpose for the church is to reach the lost so that none should perish. 2nd Peter 3:9 states, "The Lord is not slow about his promise as some count slowness, but is forbearing toward you, not wishing that any should perish, but that all should reach repentance."

The leadership has to remember John 15:5 as they constantly think about the harvest.

There is another scenario that sometimes occurs in churches that is a mystery. The leadership launches into the Great Commission. Many souls are saved and become members. Outreach is effective and the church grows. Love is present in all things, and everything seems to be going well, but growth gradually slows or stops. It is my opinion that this can happen because of several reasons.

The first reason could be that the church has become a comfortable little family, and doesn't look to God to pull them out of their comfort zone. Unspoken fears start to develop regarding a new cycle of growth.

Maybe the leaders let their guard down a little, forgetting that God will supply a reinforcement of people that will rise up to handle responsibilities in areas that are brought about by growth. In these situations I've seen the church service slow down, too. The length of the service that is comfortable for regulars can be boring to first-time visitors if it is too long. You don't have to rush, but be aware of moving forward. In my experience, most of the churches that constantly grow have a service lasting between seventy and eighty minutes.

A second reason could be forgetting the importance of home prayer groups that constantly grow and multiply; or neglecting the insistence that each group review and study the pastor's weekly message.

A third possibility may be found in service-related details. Perhaps the worship teams aren't expanding, the quality of sound isn't constantly monitored, or maybe the drama team and its humor is forgotten. I believe that powerful sermons can be supplemented with all kinds of tools and illustrations once or twice a month.

A fourth is the total surrender of the Sunday service. Is there an undercurrent of love that flows? Are the sermons the right length? The sermon length should match the urging of the Holy Spirit, and the speaker's gifted ability to communicate with each individual. Is there oneness in worship that adores our loving God in song and prayer? Do first time visitors feel comfortable? Do they return for a second and third visit? If they don't, your congregation will **rarely** invite new people. Sharing the most fun in town is the number one reason for having the problem of too many people and not enough seats.

A fifth reason for slowed or stopped growth is wolves. Sometimes a church will be doing all the right things, and will grow steadily; but then, once in a while, something just won't feel right. Time passes. You can't put your finger on it, but a series of little problems leads to grumbling from those whom you would least expect. Maybe you have a wolf. Maybe you have wolves. The Apostle Paul gave us a warning. In Acts 20:28-30 he said, "Take heed to yourselves and to all the flock, in which the Holy Spirit has made you guardians, to feed the church of the Lord which he obtained with his own blood. I know that after my departure fierce wolves will come in among you, not sparing the flock; and from among your own selves will arise men speaking perverse things, to draw away the disciples after them."

I believe that the devil will use an unsuspecting, well-meaning soul, and develop them into a wolf. This can happen when someone gets saved and uses their natural talents and desires to create a ministry in their head that doesn't come from Jesus. They bypass or ignore the results of a spiritual gifts test; and/or counsel with a trained leader. They often don't understand how the devil can win spiritual battles. Perhaps the devil tricks a person into resenting authority. Regardless of how it comes about, wolves can enter into your flock with false preconceived notions of how they are going to use their talents to serve God in your church. After a while they get frustrated and start circling the flock, picking off sheep one-by-one. The sheep start to grumble. Sometimes great damage can be done. Months later you look back and realize who the wolf was.

The Lord will bring you talented, gifted souls that are a perfect fit for service in your church. Your members were created to serve, and they are all very human, and have all the traits that go along their humanity. They will sometimes get frustrated, sad, tired, angry, and joyful. Sometimes they will vocalize their discomforts, views, and joys. That's okay, they are just people. A little grumbling is expected. It is usually outweighed a hundred times over by praises and joy, but I would caution you to learn to spot wolves.

When I hear that a church is growing, I try to attend a service and also try to ask as many people as possible why they attend this particular church. I hear the same things over and over. "The pastor talks directly to me." "This church felt comfortable the first time I visited and still does." "This church has great programs for youth."

"The music in the Praise and Worship part of the service is awesome, and isn't too loud or too soft." "The volume of the pastor's sermons is just right. I can hear clearly. It's not too loud or distorted or too soft." "The people make me feel welcome." "I can use my spiritual gifts to serve God in this church." "I'm being encouraged to serve in a job that I'm not good at yet, but I hope to be someday. One of the leaders is patiently teaching me." "My home group is wonderful. We are close. We are part of a church that Jesus uses to reach out to the lost in love." "I feel the presence of God in this church." "The service is fun."

Please note: The following five paragraphs were added about sixteen months after the initial writing of this section. The church attendance had reached nine hundred, or more, on any given Sunday.

I would like to point out that my new church, which had a little over three hundred or so parishioners not that long ago, now has one hundred fifteen Sunday school workers, and a teen ministry which is constantly growing, and right now has over one hundred fifty teens.

Numbers 12:3 states, "Now the man Moses was very meek, more than all the men that were on the face of the earth." If you talk to members who have been part of this church for several years you will find out that the pastors have long been humble servants. These folks will also tell you that it was work that was shared by many which caused each stage of growth to leap into the next.

The pastors often remind everyone to read John 15:5, and they constantly encourage us to continue in prayer and fasting, as decisions must be made at each growth plateau before moving onto the next. Our focus is not directed to what we *could* do as we reach out into our community with God's love, but rather to what we *should* do as we corporately surrender, and are guided by the Holy Spirit.

In this book I have made references to humor. Several years ago Evelyn and I drove out to Syracuse, New York to hear John Maxwell. Our friends Jewel and Jessica Pease went with us. While attending church the following Sunday, I somehow ended up on stage and was asked to describe Mr. Maxwell's talk. I said it was very powerful and funny.

Many people will tell you that in our new home church the Senior Pastor, Peter Bonanno, sets the tone for a lot of smiling and humor, and it is obvious that he has power in his life. It has taken me a long time to figure out the source of Pastor Peter's and John Maxwell's power and humor. I believe the power flows from the relationship they have with their Savior. When you see the Lord's power manifest through leadership, sermons, and relationships in the lives of these men or in the life of any Christian, you see humble surrender, exalted love, adoration, and trust. The humor comes from realizing how inadequate we humans are when we try to accomplish life's quests on our own. A great deal of their humor comes from narrating stories of their own shortcomings. They know their weaknesses, but more importantly, they know His power.

Let's look at 2nd Corinthians 12:7-10, which states, "And to keep me from being too elated by the abundance of revelations, a thorn was given me in the flesh, a messenger of Satan, to harass me, to keep me from being too elated. Three times I besought the Lord about this, that it should leave me; but he said to me, 'My grace is sufficient for you, for my power is made perfect in weakness.' I will all the more gladly boast of my weaknesses, that the power of Christ may rest upon me. For the sake of Christ, then, I am content with weaknesses, insults, hardships, persecutions, and calamities; for when I am weak, then I am strong."

The steady growth of our new church has coincided with the joining of highly qualified people that stepped up to the plate, and were put in charge of ministries within the body. God raised the ideal people to lead music ministries, Sunday school, teen ministries, divorce care, marriage counseling, outreach, small groups, ushers and greeters, cleaning, missions, lawn care, building maintenance, intercessory prayer, men's ministries, women's ministries, video productions, drama, dance, and so on. Where do you suppose all these people came from?

How the Devil Devours

Did you ever stand near the edge of a cliff or some other high place and feel a very small, sudden urge to jump off? Your common sense immediately overrides this urge, and it is soon forgotten.

Part of the tragedy of the fall of man is the imprinting that Satan left on the human mind for all generations to come. It is of a spiritual nature so those who aren't saved wouldn't understand the concept.

Matthew 4:5-6 states, "Then the devil took Him to the holy city, and set Him on the pinnacle of the temple, and said to Him, 'If you are the Son of God, throw yourself down.' " The devil was tempting Jesus.

Let's review the fall and see exactly what the enemy of your soul is up to. First he tricked Eve by suggesting doubt. Did God really say that? Genesis 3:1 reads, "He said to the woman, Did God say, 'You shall not eat of any tree of the garden?' " From doubt the devil went to deception and more tempting until she gave in and disobeyed God.

The devil can prompt us. John 13:2 states, "And during supper, when the devil had already put it into the heart of Judas Iscariot, Simon's son, to betray Him." We also see that the devil can enter into us. John 13:27 states, "Then after the morsel, Satan entered into him."

What are your hidden scrolls? What sin do you hide from Him? Is it lying, gossip, lust, greed, gluttony, licentiousness, anger, jealousy, selfishness, obsessive spending or gambling, filthy language, sexual immorality, drugs, or drunkenness? How about envy or haughtiness? Whatever it is, the devil is very real and will tempt you and taunt you so you will sin and separate yourself from God. Galatians 5:17 tells us, "For the desires of the flesh are against the Spirit, and the desires of the Spirit are against the flesh."

The devil will keep imprinting until you weaken and give him a foothold because he knows that if you do not repent and ask Jesus for help, God will give you over. Ephesians 4:26-27 commands, "Be angry but do not sin; do not let the sun go down on your anger, and give no opportunity to the devil." This means no opportunity or foothold. Isaiah 34:2 tells us, "For the Lord is enraged against all the nations, and furious against all their host, He has doomed them, has given them over for the slaughter." Romans 1:24 states, "Therefore God gave them up in the lusts of their hearts to impurity, to the dishonoring of their bodies among themselves." He gave them over. Romans 1:26 states, "For this reason God gave them up to dishonorable passions." Romans 1:28 reads, "And since they did not see fit to acknowledge God, God gave them up to a base mind and to improper conduct." God gave them over.

Once you are given over to your sin, the devil has successfully separated you from God's ways, and your mind-set has been changed to reject God, and embrace the ways of the devil. If you continue choosing to deal with it on your own and turn your back on God's ways, the enemy of your soul will devour you. In a short while, the devil will trick you into thinking that this sin is alright to do, and you will easily justify it.

Paul tells us more about a devoured soul in Romans 1:29-32, which clearly states, "They were filled with all manner of wickedness, evil, covetousness, malice. Full of envy, murder, strife, deceit, malignity, they are gossips, slanderers, haters of God, insolent, haughty, boastful, inventors of evil, disobedient to parents, foolish, faithless, heartless, ruthless. Though they know God's decree that those who do such things deserve to die, they not only do them but approve those who practice them."

Unfortunately, many choose to live in the futility of their own minds concerning the pull of the desires that are subtly engaged by their enemy. This is the second method that results in being given over. These poor souls absolutely refuse to hear the truth about sin, and give themselves over to the lusts of their sins. I have even known ministers that refuse to acknowledge that sexual practices outside marriage are sinful, and participate in such practices themselves. Ephesians 4:18 states, "they are darkened in their understanding, alienated from the life of God because of the ignorance that is in them, due to their hardness of heart; they have become callous and have given themselves up to licentiousness, greedy to practice every kind of uncleanness." The enemy tricks them with the short-term pleasure of power, and after he has seduced them into selling their souls, he destroys them.

Satan, who is your enemy, is a **spirit**. You can't see him, but you can see the effect he has on people. 1st Peter 5:8-10 warns, "Be sober and watchful. Your adversary the devil prowls around like a roaring lion, seeking some one to devour. Resist him, firm in your faith, knowing that the same experience of suffering is required of your brotherhood throughout the world. And after you have suffered a little while, the God of all grace, who has called you to his eternal glory in Christ, will himself restore, establish, and strengthen you."

Isaiah 1:28 tells us, "But rebels and sinners shall be destroyed together, and those who forsake the Lord shall be consumed." Isaiah 1:31 states, "And the strong shall become tow, and his work a spark, and both of them shall burn together, with none to quench them." In this case the word tow means broken fiber or 'tinder.' In Matthew 10:28, Jesus said, "Rather be afraid of the One who can destroy both the soul and the body in hell."

It is sad when those who are given over reject our message of love. God loves these people, but is separated from them by their stubborn pride, as they refuse to humble themselves, repent, and accept Jesus into their hearts. There is always a chance that they can be rescued and saved. We must diligently approach them with His love and show them the Truth by our love. In my life as a Christian, I have seen many who were **given over** suddenly hear our message, have a change of heart, repent, and become saved.

Spiritual Warfare

When it comes to spiritual warfare I look to the ministry of Kathryn Kuhlman. She knew the Holy Spirit and had absolute love and confidence in Jesus. The Lord blessed me as I corresponded for several years back and forth with Maggie Hartner, Kathryn's personal aide. I learned a lot. Kathryn talked about being born again, and about faith. You can't strain to get it, nor can you think it. Jesus is the answer.

Kathryn used to say that you should do all that you are supposed to do, and at the same time, give it to God in absolute surrender. In addition to owning most of her books, I have many of her radio broadcasts on cassette tapes. Though I haven't listened to any broadcasts in a long while, I hear God's voice speaking through her almost everyday just when that special time comes that I need to smile. It was like this, "As long as Almighty God is still on His throne, and He hears and answers prayer, and your faith in Him is intact, everything will be alright." Kathryn's very unique speech pattern actually sounded more like this, "As long as Almighty God is steeel on His throne, and He hears and answers prayer, and your faith in Him is intact, everything will be alllright."

Kathryn Kuhlman was humble and transparent, and had an absolute authority from God to preach. Her humble witness was evident in all of her ministry.

Ed is a close friend of mine who belongs to a small fundamental Bible study. Even though they are small, they are quite well known in our area because several of their members are noted scholars. Finding out their views on Bible passages and concepts is always fun because of the depth of their research and insight. I am usually very satisfied, and enlightened by their views and opinions.

We meet once or twice a month for oatmeal, tea, and prayer. After I started writing this section, I couldn't wait to ask him what his study group's opinion was on spiritual warfare. He told me that the fight is positional. Mark 8:33 tells us, "But turning and seeing His disciples, he rebuked Peter, and said, 'Get behind me Satan! For you are not on the side of God, but of men.' " My friend said that this is a pattern for the actual battle. Jesus was getting ready to fight. We cannot directly fight Satan because he is too powerful. We are to strongly disagree or rebuke him, and are to get in our directed position. Here we see that Satan had entered into Peter with imprinting of fear and deception, and Peter was reacting. Jesus separated His disciples from the accuser. This would mean that it is us, Jesus in the middle, and then Satan.

Each time we meet I am full of questions, and my friend is full of answers that I value and investigate. In this case, it is one of the few times that I would like to go directly to my friend's meeting to discuss the issue further. I don't totally disagree, but I would like to talk this out because the incident above happened before Christ took His place at the right hand of the Father, and before He sent the Holy Spirit to live in His followers.

My recollection of Ms. Kuhlman's many references to battles with the enemy almost seemed to come from a perspective that we are to take a more active role of awareness and action in our daily lives. Kathryn certainly warned repeatedly to beware of the enemy of your soul, but always pointed to Jesus for victory. You must learn to recognize the devil's tactics but don't blame the devil for all of your problems. Have gumption in your quests and live in Christ.

Colossians 1:16 states, "for in Him all things were created in heaven and on earth, visible and invisible, whether thrones or dominions or principalities or authorities...all things were created through Him and for Him." The spirit world is mostly beyond the realm of human understanding. But Jesus totally understands the spiritual realm, for He created it! I know my Savior. The more you learn to surrender to Him, the more you will realize His power in your life.

In the early eighties, I investigated many claims people made about defeating the devil in spiritual warfare. I traveled far and wide to watch what these people were doing first hand. Many tried to scream and bind Satan, many tried to cast out demons in various ways, and many said that they were stomping on Satan, and crushing him. I did extensive follow-ups and ended up not believing a word of it. It is my opinion that they had two problems: They didn't understand scripture, and they went beyond the authority given to them by Jesus.

For instance, one night I drove a friend to a mid-week meeting about an hour away featuring a preacher that would 'Rid you' of demons. The church that was sponsoring the traveling preacher started the whole affair with ten minutes of rousing music led by their worship team. Then the guest preacher walked to the front waving a Bible. He was very loud and quoted a lot of scripture. People with all manner of problems went up front and sat in a chair as he danced around and screamed the demons out of them. He told all who would listen that he had his demon-stomping boots on. He obviously did not have the authority from Jesus as my followup revealed no actual healings.

Weeks later, in my very own home town, there was a lot of talk about a family who recently moved in and claimed to cast out demons. It took quite a few phone calls before I located them. I invited them over to my house. They walked in with Bibles and two-foot-high crosses. We talked for a while and prayed, and then they boldly burst into each room of the house, holding up the crosses and yelling at the demons. They were cleaning house for me. Back then I didn't get the whole picture of a lot that was going on. I didn't understand wise and prudent use of money or the blessings you will receive when you generously give in ways that glorify God. Many years of intermittent, financial struggles have taught me to be humble, but during that time period business had been good for a few years and pride came into the equation. Part of being puffed up with myself was the gold ring with a diamond that I sported on my right hand. Mind you, its okay to have a ring, but mine was worn for all the wrong, prideful reasons. Somehow, during the whole demon-casting experience they convinced me that demons resided in the ring and took it with them to... 'Melt it down.'

I sat down the next evening, wrote Maggie a short note, and asked her what Kathryn had said about demons. She quickly replied and said she didn't remember ever hearing Kathryn mention them.

God is sovereign, and hears and answers heart-felt prayer. He often heals people, but we must be humble and give all glory to Him. A few months ago it pleased the Lord to miraculously heal me. He heard my pleas asking for healing from asthma, which had afflicted me for more than 30 years. My doctor sent me for pulmonary function testing because I was convinced of my complete healing and wanted to jettison all of my asthma medication. I keep the test results in my glove compartment verifying that I am now asthma free. The document reminds me daily of His mercy and power.

There seems to be no argument in the modern day times in which we live as to the effectiveness of God's work through Kathryn Kuhlman. Thousands and thousands were, and still are, led to be born again into the kingdom of God through her work. And there seems to be no doubt in my mind that documented healings occurred in this work more than in any other ministry since the Bible was written. Let's look at Mark 3:14, which tells us, "And he appointed twelve, to be with him, and to be sent out to preach and have authority to cast out demons:" Kathryn well understood the prerequisite that was needed to get the job done...to **be** with Jesus. She humbled herself, was sent with authority to preach, and gave Him all the glory. She was given knowledge at the very moment when the Holy Spirit was healing people. God knows the spirit of each of us in detail. He gives a blessing of gifts and knowledge to those who will use and not abuse them. I have observed that the more generously you use your gifts to humbly serve God and man—the more He will bless your walk with

Power.

The devil is constantly trying to control human minds. His primary motive, of course, is to trick and deceive us so we won't choose to be born again. He knows that if we are truly born again we will become a temple of the Living God, the Holy Spirit will live in us, and God's Kingdom will come to earth in our hearts. The devil pays particular attention to members of churches so the church will be rendered useless in winning souls for Christ.

For six thousand years, many cultures and religions have been ingrained with stories of floods, virgin births, and false gods. It is my belief that the originators of these stories and gods were influenced by the enemy to build a case against the Truth. I think that it would be impossible to come to this conclusion if one had not traveled into the other spiritual dimension in their journey.

Deception and negativity toward God's values and truths has always been used to separate man from God. The enemy of your soul is constantly influencing people to create false doctrine, false interpretations, and even blatant changes in Biblical text so as to incubate lust, fear, and pride. Satan is a liar and is out to destroy you.

We have many accounts in the Bible of societies that sacrificed their children to false gods. Evil is easily justified in the spiritual dimension of the devil. Several of Israel's kings blended with local cultures, adopted false gods, and sacrificed their own children in the fire. Take a good look at history and see what happens when people turn their back on God. Psalm 81:11&12 shows us, "But my people did not listen to my voice; Israel would have none of me. So I gave them over to their stubborn hearts, to follow their own counsels."

It was a long time ago when I last listened to any of Ms. Kuhlman's radio programs on tape and I don't remember all that she said about gumption but I knew that our fight in spiritual warfare was talked about in Ephesians and I waited on the Lord to give me more information.

Ephesians 6:10-11 instructs us, "Finally, be strong in the Lord in the strength of His might. Put on the whole armor of God, that you may be able to stand against the wiles of the devil." Verses 14-18 continue, "Stand therefore, having girded your loins with truth, and having put on the breastplate of righteousness, and having shod your feet with the equipment of the gospel of peace; above all taking the shield of faith, with which you can quench all the flaming darts of the evil one. And take the helmet of salvation, and the sword of the Spirit, which is the word of God. Pray at all times in the Spirit, with all prayer and supplication."

The Lord blessed me in my new home church as they had just started a four-part series on spiritual warfare. After listening a few Sundays to Senior Pastor Peter Bonanno, and one Sunday to Pastor Lisa Bonanno talk about the subject, I realized that their messages contained the information I was looking for. Both pastors believe, as Kathryn Kuhlman did, that you have to take an active stance against the enemy of your soul, and do your part in the fight, while at the same time, totally surrendering to God. As these two pastors put it, "Take your position **in** Christ."

The first part of the series was, 'You have an enemy: Spiritual warfare is not just an idea, it's reality.' Pastor Peter started by talking about the modern world's perception of the devil. "There is this subtle downplaying of the dark side, kind of like making it acceptable. The truth is...we have watered down the devil. He doesn't exist. He's this guy who wanders around in a red suit, with horns, a tail, and a pitchfork. That's how we think of the devil." He went on to say that the devil is real. We shouldn't be afraid of him, but rather expose him.

His sermon taught how to recognize Satan's lies and deceptions, and that there is a real battle. He said, "The **devil's biggest weapon** against us is ignorance about his existence, and ignorance about the battle we need to fight. What are you facing today? You may be facing a difficulty in your marriage, you may be facing a difficulty in your finances, or you may be facing a difficulty in your prayer life. Let me tell you. You have a battle, and you have an enemy. This is not just happening because it's God's will. God's will is for you to fight, and for you to stand against the enemy of your soul. Remember, the enemy doesn't want anything more for you than to steal from you, to kill you, and to destroy you. This lesson is for you to see the war. We sometimes don't, and we back off, and give up."

It was an early morning service, but I was starting to get fully awake. He said, "You can't make a peace treaty with the enemy. He won't leave you alone. He hates you. You can't ignore that he exists, and think, 'I'll be okay.' The only way to be okay is this..." and he quoted from 1st John 4:4, which reads, "for he who is in you is greater than he who is in the world." Then he said,, "When you gravitate toward lust or anger or self, remember, you have an enemy." Ephesians 6:12 states, "For we are not contending against flesh and blood, but against the principalities, against the powers, against the world rulers of this present darkness, against the spiritual hosts of wickedness in heavenly places."

Pastor Peter then told us why the devil is our enemy. It is because there is a glory in our life that the enemy fears. He is bent on destroying your life before your work can come to fruition. A long time ago his pride got him thrown out of heaven. He wanted to be like God. Revelation 12:7-9 states, "Now a war arose in heaven, Michael and his angels fighting against the dragon; and the dragon and his angels fought, but they were defeated and there was no longer any place for them in heaven. And the great dragon was thrown down, that ancient serpent, who is called the Devil and Satan, the deceiver of the whole world—he was thrown down to the earth, and his angels were thrown down with him."

Pastor Peter further directed, "Look at what happens in Revelation 12:10-12, "Now the salvation and the power and the kingdom of our God and the authority of his Christ have come, for the accuser of our brethren has been thrown down, who accuses them day and night before our God. And they have conquered him by the blood of the Lamb and by the word of their testimony, for they loved not their lives unto death. Rejoice then, O heaven and you that dwell therein! But woe to you, O earth and sea, for the devil has come down to you in great wrath, because he knows that his time is short." And from verse 17: "Then the dragon was angry with the woman, and went off to make war on the rest of her offspring, on those who keep the commandments of God and bear testimony to Jesus." "

Pastor Lisa preached the second part of the series. She talked about mind games that the enemy plays on us. First she reminded us that the devil does not live in hell. He is roaming the earth and is a powerful spiritual force in his dominion. He will try to get you to believe that Christ doesn't love you or that you don't have a purpose in life.

She said, "The key area that the enemy targets is our mind. If he can control our thoughts about ourselves, God, and other people, he can defeat us because he can then control our actions. He doesn't play fair. He plays against our weaknesses, our past, our insecurities, or our mindset about people. These are some examples. I'm just going to read them off:

- Why bother trusting anyone, people will always let you down.
- All men are alike. They only want to use you.
- All women are out to destroy men and take control. You just can't trust them.
- You failed, you big loser, just give up.
- You're a terrible mom. Your kids are going to be messed up.
- You poor thing, nobody cares for you. They don't even notice that you exist. Just give in to this desire, no one will ever know."

Pastor Lisa went on to say that the enemy is the father of lies. The examples that she read were just a small fraction of the lies he hits us with. She showed us through scripture how the devil uses a little truth and mixes it with lies so as to trick and destroy us.

Then she moved on to the fight. Second Corinthians 10:3-5 states, "For though we live in the world we are not carrying on a worldly war, for the weapons of our warfare are not worldly but have divine power to destroy strongholds. We destroy arguments and every proud obstacle to the knowledge of God, and take every thought captive to obey Christ." She explained that in this passage Paul is telling us not to believe everything the enemy says, but take captive and examine every thought. She said, "We also have to learn to discern strongholds. A stronghold is anything that exalts itself in our minds, pretending to be bigger and more powerful than God. It ends up being a strong hold that ends up holding us. These could be attitudes that we have such as guilt over some poor choices that we may have made in the past. Unforgiveness can be a big stronghold. When you get hurt in a relationship, and hold on to that hurt, it becomes part of you. Pride can also be a stronghold."

Then she told us, "Your strongholds can feed on themselves and open the door for deeper strongholds such as addictions. Food, alcohol, drugs, pornography, and being consumed with worry and fear are all areas that the enemy of your soul wants you to hold on to. Instead, you should talk to God. Identify, confess, and surrender. Strongholds will take your eyes off the Lord, and keep you defeated and discouraged. Satan will talk to us all the time and say, 'You'll never be free. You'll never be free.' That's a lie of the enemy."

As I sat there listening to her, and writing as fast as I could, I thought of Joel Osteen saying, "Don't take ownership of that problem!" And I thought of Kathryn Kuhlman saying: "Just give it to Jesus!"

Pastor Lisa proceeded to point out that the enemy will also use strongholds to make your family miserable. She said, "Satan will not only destroy your household, but will project fear and disorder into your children. The Lord wants you to run to Him, not toward that weakness that is being held. She said that a teenager may hold on to grief and despair, feel unloved, and go find anything to replace that feeling because they don't understand the spiritual battle. We must teach them that we love them, and that God loves them, and how to have victory in Jesus."

This is a very serious subject, and portrayed that way, but I would like to note that Pastor Peter, Pastor Lisa, Kevin Hardy, Joel Osteen, and Kathryn Kuhlman were blessed with the ability to weave in appropriate humor. Usually this humor is directed at their own shortcomings. I have seen people of all ages, especially teens, identify with and learn from these people.

The sermon continued with her describing the peace that can come about in any situation that is brought to the Lord. She told a serious story about feeling rejected on her birthday, and then said that after she had a good long cry, she laid it at the Lord's feet. He revealed a **stronghold** from her past which was fear of rejection, and He came in with peace and healing and spoke to her heart. John 8:32 states, "and you will know the truth, and the truth will make you free." Lisa paraphrased Zephaniah 3:17 " 'He quiets me with His love, and He sings over me;' " then said, "God loves you and is proud that you are His son or daughter. He wants to set us free by giving us His truth, the truth about how He sees us, and His purpose for us." You could feel the healing love sweeping through the congregation.

She mentioned Isaiah 26:3, which says, "Thou dost keep him in perfect peace, whose mind is stayed on thee," and made a suggestion to anyone that had never accepted Jesus to think about doing so now.

This had been an early morning service. I went home and straight to my office. After I corrected scribbles in my notes that were fresh in my mind, I started rifling through my pondering pile. It's about a foot high and contains quotes, partially written songs, and thoughts.

I flipped through the scraps of paper, trying not to let any fall on the floor. Then I found it. On a torn, faded yellow, lined piece of notebook paper I had written a quote that I had heard on the radio. There evidently hadn't been time to pull over and record the speaker's name. This piece of paper has been well handled over the ten or so years it had been in the pile. It reads, "God's healing can begin when you allow Him to come in and love you."

In the third part of the series Pastor Peter answered the question: If the battle is the Lord's, why fight? He also talked about strategy for winning. He described spiritual warfare as the antidote for when the enemy comes against us. We have to surrender to the Lord again and again and again.

The pastor started with facts about the enemy. He said, "Satan is very subtle. He is not like a bully that we can see. He comes at us when we have our guard down, when we are vulnerable. Luke 4:13 tells us, 'And when the devil had ended every temptation, he departed from him until an opportune time.' " He said that the devil would wait until perhaps a time when Jesus was more vulnerable. "That's what Satan does in our lives. He's cunning and deceptive. Can the devil read our minds? No, he doesn't have to. He can see your attitudes, your actions, and responses."

Pastor Peter went on to say, "This is not a series designed to give you nightmares." He said that he didn't want people to be paranoid and walk around thinking: 'Is he out to get me?' It is important, however, that you should be aware that there are certain extremes when it comes to spiritual warfare. "One extreme is that we are so afraid and worried that we don't even bother to fight."

He said, "In some Christian circles there is an erroneous teaching that you should only go against Satan with a very specific formula with certain words. I think that this leads a believer to fear. We are seated in Christ, and have a way to come against the enemy. Another extreme is to walk around oblivious to the power of the enemy, thinking that if you mention Satan's name you'll give him more power. Some say we give the dark side power by admitting our weaknesses, or by revealing a stronghold, thinking that: 'Now he sees it and will play it against me.' The reality is that when you confess your sins, and when you are openly transparent, the truth sets us free. These other ways cause displaced fear, and are unhealthy. We should enter the fight and fear God not Satan."

The pastor then talked about and explained Acts 19:11-20, which reads, "And God did extraordinary miracles by the hand of Paul, so that handkerchiefs or aprons were carried away from his body to the sick and diseases left them and the evil spirits came out of them. Then some of the itinerant Jewish exorcists undertook to pronounce the name of the Lord Jesus over those who had evil spirits, saying, 'I adjure you by the Jesus whom Paul preaches.'

Seven sons of a Jewish high priest named Sceva were doing this. But the evil spirit answered them, 'Jesus I know, and Paul I know; but who are you?' And the man in whom the evil spirit was leaped on them, and overpowered them, so that they fled out of the house naked and wounded.

And this became known to all residents of Ephesus, both Jews and Greeks; and fear fell upon them all; and the name of the Lord Jesus was extolled. Many of those who were now believers came, confessing and divulging their practices. And a number of those who practiced magic arts brought their books (scrolls) together and burned them in the sight of all; and they counted the value of them and found it came to fifty thousand pieces of silver. So the word of the Lord prevailed mightily." (Please note: I inserted the parentheses and the word (scrolls) because in the pastor's Bible the text used the word scrolls. The Revised Standard Version that I have quoted uses the word (books)).

The pastor told us to note that the believers in the story were overcome with fear. Many of them confessed their practices. They had scrolls, or books, of their sorcery hidden from the Lord. They came out from their hiding and keeping things in secret from God. The more we hide, the more the enemy has to hold over us. When we confess our sins, the devil will flee. We also see here that the word spread about Jesus **when** believers got right with God.

His sermon continued, "The seven sons wanted attention. They wanted to be great in the eyes of men. They may have even wanted to help people, so they started using Jesus' name. The Bible says that the evil spirit didn't recognize them, and overpowered them because Jesus wasn't really in them, so the demons had no fear. The evil spirit gave them such a beating that they ran out of the house naked and bleeding. They were unbelievers that were suffering from terrible bondage from the enemy. Without Jesus in your heart there is no hope to be set free."

He said, "Here God has given us a window into the spiritual world that will give us greater and lasting victory over the enemy. We defeat Satan, not by ignoring him, not by rebuking him, but by fearing God. When we fear God, Satan and his demons lose every time." The pastor paraphrased from Luke 10:19-20 saying: "They came back, and said, Even the demons obey us, and Jesus said, Don't rejoice at that, but rejoice that your names are written in heaven, that you have a relationship with God." Fear God, submit, and praise Him. The enemy will lose and you will win.

Someone had come to Pastor Peter after the first message in the series and asked, "If the battle is the Lord's, why even fight?" The pastor explained that in the Bible there are verses that tell us our position in Christ, and to be active. Timothy 6:12 states, "**Fight** the good fight of faith." Ephesians 6:10 says, "**be strong** in the Lord and in the strength of his might." 6:11 tells us, "**Put on** the whole armor of God." "… **stand firm** against the wiles of the devil." He went on talking about the active part we are to take in the battle, and emphasized action phrases such as "**put on** the breastplate of righteousness" and "**take** the helmet of salvation and the sword of the Spirit." (Please note that

I have taken the liberty of bolding the words to parallel the pastor's emphasis on them.)

The pastor then gave us the meaning of a passage I had wondered about for years. Matthew 18:18 states, "Truly, I say to you, whatever you bind on earth shall be bound in heaven, and whatever you loose on earth shall be loosed in heaven." He said, "This shows that our part is not to sit back and do nothing. There is an active part that we play. God puts the initiative into the hands of His people, and **He promises** that when we fight in the Spirit of the Lord, heaven moves!"

He then redirected our focus back to the scrolls and challenged us. He asked, **"What scrolls do you have hidden from the Lord?"** He nudged us to examine ourselves, and see what we are trying to hide from God. He said that people don't talk about fearing God enough. **The devil fears God** and will run away from us when we bring our dark areas into the light. Only when we first submit our lives openly to the Lord can we **resist** the enemy and win the battle.

The **fourth** part of the series was about a better time. Satan's pattern can be discovered as we look into the Word. He pushes our buttons, plays off our weaknesses, and tempts us in our hungers. The title of the message was 'How Long?'

Pastor Peter said that after you become a Christian you tend to look at things differently. One of the things he pointed out is that we can look at life as a series of circumstances, and feel that we are victims of those circumstances. This builds on the fact that there are experiences in our past that sometimes haunt us. As Christians, these circumstances do not have to define who we are today.

The enemy has a tactic to stir up things from our past. He quoted 2nd Corinthians 2:11, part of which reads, "…for we are not ignorant of his designs." And then the pastor said, "The enemy can trick us into thinking that bad things that have happened to us can reoccur, and can cause us to fear today, and in the future. A multitude of irrational or unnecessary fears can develop and control our thoughts and lives.

The old wounds can become part of our identity. We can become overly and unnecessarily cautious about living today, and planning tomorrow. Our thoughts can be tied to negative experiences in our past. If we aren't careful we can pass these fears on to our children. We need to learn to recognize the devil's ways, and we need to be delivered."

Our main scripture was from Mark 9. A man brought his son to Jesus' disciples to see if the boy could be healed of the demon that held him in bondage. When the demon seized him it dashed him down, and in Mark 9:18 the Scripture says, "and wherever it seizes him, it dashes him down; and he foams and grinds his teeth and becomes rigid; and I asked your disciples to cast it out, and they were not able." The disciples were unable to heal him. Verses 20-29 continue, "And they brought the boy to Him, immediately it convulsed the boy, and he fell on the ground and rolled about, foaming at the mouth. And Jesus asked his father, 'How long has he had this?' And he said, 'From childhood. And it has often cast him into the fire and into the water, to destroy him; but if you can do anything, have pity on us and help us.' And Jesus said to him, 'If you can! (The original Greek says, "If thou art able to believe.") All things are possible to him who believes.' Immediately the father of the child cried out and said, 'I believe; help my unbelief!' And when Jesus saw that a crowd came running together, he rebuked the unclean spirit, saying to it, 'You dumb and deaf spirit, I command you, come out of him, and never enter him again.' And after crying out and convulsing him terribly, it came out, and the boy was like a corpse; so that most of them said, 'He is dead.' But Jesus took him by the hand and lifted him up, and he arose. And when he had entered the house, his disciples asked him privately, 'Why could we not cast it out?' And he said to them, 'This kind cannot be driven out by anything but prayer.' " (The original Greek says 'prayer and fasting.')

Pastor Peter asks, "What is the significance of what Jesus is saying here? Look at verse twenty-one. Jesus asked the boy's father, 'How long has he been like that?' Was that just small talk?" The pastor then related the situation to hypothetical scenarios that might occur in our lives. "**How long** have you struggled with that? How long have you been in that job that you don't like? How long have you been married to that guy? This is a key to our struggles with the evil one. How long has it been? God can deliver us in a moment. There is no doubt about that. Look at the power of the Cross. That's what it means to be an old creation, and then become a new creation in Christ. We need to see the fiery darts of the enemy. Many times that dart is to drudge up our past, throw it in our face, and to make us think, that is who we are, and that's who we will always be."

He went on, "There have been sins in our life that have separated us from God; no doubt about that. There have been hurts that have happened that made us think that God wasn't concerned, and we have said, 'Where is God?' The Bible calls Satan the accuser. He's like this little (no offense to attorneys intended) bad attorney that stands before God, and he says, 'Look at how they failed. How can you love them?' The accuser says, 'Give me some options here,' just like he did in the book of Job. He is diabolical. This word comes from the Greek word for the devil. It means: 'a false accuser prone to slander.' " Then the pastor told us that it's not just that Satan accuses us before God, but also he accuses God before us. We looked at what the serpent said to Eve.

He said, "The devil plants accusations and doubts, such as, 'Are you sure God really forgave you?' In our text from Mark, Satan may have come to the man and said, 'Nothing is going to help now.' So the man said to Jesus, 'If you can....' "

Our pastor then asked, "What has the enemy been whispering to you? In what way has he accused you before God? In what way has he accused God before you? Is there something in your life so deep, some pain that you just can't let go of? Some fear you can't trust God with? In fact, you keep dredging that fear up over and over again? Maybe you fear that you will repeat something from the past, or maybe some memory that is raw, and is always there on the surface. A past hurt that has defined you, and you say, 'That's who I am.' You may not say it, but you think it. Satan will get you to believe any small lie to make you think that can't get free. The devil will try to destroy your self-confidence by getting you to buy any small lie that he is selling, and accept it as normal. How long have you been like this, and believed you were a bad parent, or believed that you were incompetent?"

Our pastor told us, "God helps us discern the lies of the enemy by learning the truth in His Word. The devil might say to you, 'Look at the people around you, they're having more fun than you are. You can't enjoy life like they can. They're having conversations that relate to each other, and are fun. They're more likeable than you are.' If you buy that, the devil can then get vicious, 'People see right through you.' He can exhaust you like you are in a wrestling match. Here's the truth; you don't have to lose the wrestling match. When these things happen, learn to recognize that these thoughts are not the voice of your Shepherd. Jesus would invite you to come, and sit on His lap, and tell you that you are complete in Him."

And then he said, "When Satan comes on you, and dredges up the past, you don't have to agree with him that you are all these things today. You can agree that bad incidents may have happened, but now you are a new creature in Christ and you are not like that any more. Take your position **in** Christ. Your past sins, failures, and wounds are not part of your present or your future. Determine that they are not baggage that you carry around with you. Don't give in and say, 'This is who I am, and this is who I'll always be.'"

The pastor continued, "You need to fight. Sometimes fighting is messy, but be willing to fight. Don't give up and let the enemy win. The enemy might say, 'Don't forgive; you'll open yourself up to more hurt.' We can hold on to a hurt or bitterness because it seems comfortable. Don't accept fate as if God can't intervene and change things. **How long** have you been like this? We can't erase the past, and we may occasionally fail and fall, but we need to know what God says about us today. We overcome the enemy by the blood of the Lamb, and by the word of our testimony [describing where He has brought us from]. The devil uses the same paths in our minds over and over to defeat us. Know where these paths are and ask God to heal you there. God has a future and a plan for you and it's not dependent on the past." The pastor concluded with a quote from 1ˢᵗ John 4:4, which states, "for he who is **in** you is greater than he who is in the world." (Please note: The bolding of the word **in** is mine to reflect the pastor's emphasis.)

Please understand that in writing about these sermons I left out the stories. When Pastor Peter preaches he frequently and appropriately weaves in true stories from his life that are very funny. I would like to briefly mention one of the stories from this sermon. He told us about a mole that was ruining his backyard. The mole had created a series of tunnels and would make little entrances here and there at the

end of these pathways, or runs. These entrances were little unsightly piles of dirt, which emerged all over the place. The mole would use these runs over and over again to get his food, destroying the lawn in the process. Pastor Peter learned how to do battle with the mole. It was very funny. In the end he equated the runs of the mole with the runs of the devil, going over and over again in our minds, to reinforce negatives that keep us in bondage about the same subjects.

Sitting in the congregation and listening is not only educational and pleasant, but during the whole time he is preaching you can feel the presence of God. Love and warmth surround all who are in the church. I must also note that when he senses that someone is hurting, he can redirect his attention, and become appropriately serious, quickly.

The Thimble and the Ocean

Kathryn Kuhlman used to say that whether life grinds a man down or polishes him depends on what he's made of. She said that just as friction polishes a diamond, man is perfected by life's trials. Great pilots are made in rough waters and deep seas. You can permit the storms of life to defeat you, or use them for the glory of God. Don't wave the white flag of defeat. Ask God to take care of things that are bigger than you are.

She was a firm believer that work was valuable in keeping life's problems at bay. She also thought that keeping busy was the best cure when you had one of those days when you felt a little out of sorts. She would say, "Wwwork it off, honey!" She talked often about rewards in heaven. She believed that those who diligently serve and trust God will qualify for oceans of rewards when they reach heaven.

Each of us has obligations that can seem overwhelming at times, but I firmly believe that if you ask Him for help, you will easily find the time and energy to serve Him. We must learn to achieve a balance of work and proper rest. However, in my case, it's all too easy to flop down on the couch and grab the remote. For this reason, I keep a thimble in my briefcase. When I feel like I'm being attacked by the 'Big L' (Laziness), I pull out the thimble. It gets me back to work. I don't want to settle for a thimble full of rewards for all of eternity, just because I chose to be lazy here. I want to go to Jesus, following John 15:5, and do the best I can. I want to strive for the oceans category.

Second Chronicles 15:7 states, "But you, take courage! Do not let your hands be weak, for your work shall be rewarded." John 12:26 states, "if anyone serves me, the Father will honor him."

Seriously

When I accepted Jesus, I went to church three times a week. I climbed a small mountain near my home almost every afternoon for many weeks, and read the Bible from Genesis to Revelation to learn as much as possible about the One to whom we surrender. I was on the road for a company at the time, and listened to Christian radio off and on all day. During the first four years that I was saved, I probably listened to well over five thousand sermons.

Twenty-five years later, I now don't have enough fingers and toes to add up all the sermons I've listened to. That brings us to doctrine. You will find Bible-believing denominations that have very specific rules about who should become an elder. Others have very specific rules about who should become a deacon. Some just have board members.

I have eaten many meals with pastors and missionaries when wine was served with dinner. Conversely, there are some denominations where any kind of alcohol is strictly forbidden.

Some Bible-believing denominations encourage women to become associate pastors, and have a substantial role in leadership. You will find other Bible-believing denominations that won't let a woman teach. Some denominations allow a woman to teach or become a member of the board or become a deacon, but not become a pastor. You can observe that women do not speak at all in some services, and you will find other churches in which women must have their heads covered.

Divorce is a major issue. Some churches deny divorced people leadership roles, and others are just the opposite, and you will find that the head pastor has been divorced. There are denominations that won't marry a couple because either or both of them have been divorced, and other churches that will.

I've visited so many church services that, in many instances, it's hard to arrive unnoticed. A couple of years ago I had spent several Sundays with loved ones in an Assembly of God church, and was very comfortable dancing before the Lord during the worship part of the service. One Sunday, shortly thereafter, I was in a Nazarene church. They have doctrine against dancing. When the praise and worship started I couldn't keep my feet still. I danced around all over the place. Many folks were laughing, some so hard they had tears running down their cheeks. Weeks later I visited the same church. Many people turned to me and smiled when the music started to see if I would break the rules again. I didn't. It must be said that in each of these churches you could feel an enormous amount of love.

God has led me to services in which I think every soul in the room had their hands raised in absolute surrender to their Maker. You could feel love filling the church. In other churches I've sat in the middle of a congregation when no one raised their hands, except me, of course. And it's just like that.

Each denomination takes their doctrine very seriously, and doctrine is under constant review and study. It's obvious that sometimes they change their stance on different passages in the Bible. This comes about only as a result of many discussions, lengthy examinations, and prayer. We must respect each other's doctrine, and we must learn to work together. The enemy wants to separate us from God and from each other any way he can. We need to rise above our minor differences and the devil's urgings. Jesus commanded us to love, and wants us to be united in one voice as we reach out to the lost.

Ephesians 4:1-8 states, "I therefore, a prisoner for the Lord, beg you to lead a life worthy of the calling to which you have been called, with all lowliness and meekness, with patience, forbearing one another in love, eager to maintain the unity of the Spirit in the bond of peace. There is one body and one Spirit, just as you were called to the one hope that belongs to your call, one Lord, one faith, one baptism, one God and Father of us all, who is above all and through all and in all. But grace was given to each of us according to the measure of Christ's gift. Therefore it is said, 'When He ascended on high He led a host of captives, and He gave gifts to men.' " Ephesians 4:11-16 tells us, "And His gifts were that some should be apostles, some prophets, some evangelists, some pastors and teachers, for the equipment of the saints, for the work of ministry, for building up the body of Christ, until we all attain to the unity of the faith and of the knowledge of the Son of God, to mature manhood, to the measure of the stature of the fullness of Christ; so that we may no longer be children, tossed to and fro and carried about with every wind of doctrine, by the cunning of men, by their craftiness in deceitful wiles. Rather speaking the truth in love, we are to grow up in every way into Him who is the head, into Christ, from whom the whole body, joined and knit together by every joint with which it is supplied, when each part is working properly, makes bodily growth and up builds itself in love."

In John 13:34-35, Jesus says, "A new commandment I give to you, that you love one another; even as I have loved you, that you also love one another. By this all men will know that you are my disciples, if you have love for one another." Please notice the word 'commandment.'

For decades my Savior has often sent me to meet with people who willingly share various opinions of different scriptures that shape their views on doctrine. These experiences helped me understand the cause and effect of various attitudes on church growth.

Today we have the luxury of readily available materials to study history. It is my opinion that ongoing mindsets in the leadership of a church about denominational doctrine or regarding individual right or wrong behavior have often, in the past two thousand years, been shifted from educating, encouraging, and equipping to enforcing and controlling. It seems to me that heartfelt service to God can be in jeopardy when an attitude of control replaces an attitude of leading and encouraging.

It is clear to me that in these situations, loving man and loving

God and making disciples has been set aside. It has been replaced with a dominant preponderance of actions that simulate *dispensing* God and *dispensing* guilt. I believe that in instances like this, the congregation usually responds negatively and does not enjoy inviting friends to church. To me, the flock slips into a preoccupation with trying to figure out why they are uncomfortable. In the meantime, loyal followers patiently wait for things to get better. Sometimes they wait for decades. I personally see this type of leadership as yielding to enemy temptation, and think of it as a trap laid by the devil. In my opinion church leaders at all levels must be aware of this trap so that no degree of it creeps into the church.

Another point, if you will...let's talk about the word response. Over and over I have seen parishioners respond to leadership in very positive ways when encouraged to read the Bible daily, develop personal prayer habits [while seeking God's will], serve in their chosen purpose, and join small groups.

When a soul is born again and yields to God's will in the process of sanctification, and starts learning how to empty themselves as a vessel to be used for God's work, the Holy Spirit brings the freedom of living in Christ. The very Spirit of Jesus is evident in their actions. The more Jesus indwells souls...the more they live in freedom. Encouraging this freedom produces fruit. You will see people that are compelled to tell others about their relationship with God, their small group, and their church. Freedom equals testimony and love! Control equals frustration and quiet suspicion.

The following passages deserve consideration:

Isaiah 9:6 states, "For to us a child is born, to us a son is given, and the government will be on his shoulder, and his name will be called 'Wonderful Counselor, Mighty God, Everlasting Father, Prince of Peace.'"

In Isaiah 11:1-3 we read, "There shall come forth a shoot from the stump of Jesse, and a branch shall grow out of his roots. And the Spirit of the Lord shall rest on him, the spirit of wisdom and understanding, the spirit of counsel and might, the spirit of knowledge and the fear of the Lord. And his delight shall be in the fear of the Lord."

Hebrews 8:6-10 tells us, "But as it is, Christ has obtained a ministry which is as much more excellent than the old as the covenant he mediates is better since it is enacted on better promises. For if that first covenant had been faultless, there would have been no occasion for a second. For he finds fault with them when he says: 'The days will come, says the Lord, when I will establish a new covenant with the house of Israel and with the house of Judah; not like the covenant that I made with their fathers on the day when I took them by the hand to lead them out of the land of Egypt; for they did not continue in my covenant, and so I paid no heed to them, says the Lord. This is the covenant that I will make with the house of Israel after those days, says the Lord: I will put my laws into their minds, and write them on their hearts, and I will be their God, and they shall be my people.' "

Please note 1st Corinthians 11:25, which states, "In the same way also the cup, after supper saying, 'This cup is the new covenant in my blood. Do this, as often as you drink it in remembrance of me.' "

Psalm 133

Psalm 133 states, "Behold, how good and pleasant it is when brothers dwell in unity! It is like the precious oil upon the head, running down upon the beard, upon the beard of Aaron, running down the collar of his robes! It is like the dew of Hermon, which falls on the mountains of Zion! For there the Lord has commanded the blessing, life for evermore."

It was early on a Thursday morning. I had just left my reading group when two businessmen spotted my journaling book. They were pleasantly surprised. They told me that they were Baptists and belonged to a Foursquare journaling group in their hometown in Vermont.

The Foursquare churches have a daily Bible reading Journal that is excellent, and provides a great format for living in God's word. It also opens the door for Christians of different denominations to have fellowship on a whole different level. If you have one of their churches in your town, give them a call and check it out. If not, you can contact their headquarters at foursquare.org. The Journals are inexpensive. You could invite neighboring churches to join you.

Secrets

Secret number one: When a friend or relative comes to you, and asks for prayer, the best thing to do is pray. We, in our human trait, have a little hidden desire to lift ourselves up as knowing all the answers. Unless this person specifically asks for advice, in an area in which you have knowledge...just pray.

Secret number two: Listen. Problems in marriage, problems in business, problems in church, and most other problems in life can only be solved when you learn to listen. There is a special solution triangle that should always be tried first when solving problems. Both parties need to sit side-by-side, that's two points of the triangle, and examine the problem together. I would even recommend writing the problem on a piece of paper, place it on a table in front of both parties, and look at it. The problem itself represents the third point of the triangle. This is a much better system than examining each other. And by the way...listen.

Secret number three: You are not alone. After you are born again Jesus will guide your quest to learn to listen to your Maker and serve Him. He will give you the Holy Spirit.

When I was first saved, I tried to do too much by myself, not realizing that I should slow down and rely on Jesus for help. I struggled for a long time before learning to ask Him for guidance, seek counsel from trusted Godly people, and learning God's ways by daily Bible reading. I did it my way. I read the whole Bible through by myself, and then tried to figure out what to do next.

Without understanding what was happening, I started paying attention to the thoughts of certain new people in my life. Dave Adams, Glaphre Gilliland, Maggie Hartner, Dale Parry, and Doug Tunney all steered me in the right direction. They gave me good advice. It started with Dave helping me to understand my job, and convincing me to make a serious commitment. Then, Glaphre taught me how to get out of the box I was in, and how to cast my fears upon Jesus. Next was Maggie who kept reminding me I wasn't alone. Dale put me on a path of learning how to surrender, and Doug got me deeply into a Biblical perspective, and daily reading. It was years before I put two and two together. God had caused the contacts that nurtured my direction.

Take a look at Luke 9:23, which reads, "And he said to all, 'If any man would come after me, let him deny himself and take up his cross daily and follow me.' " The cross was heavy. I kept falling down, and try as I might, I couldn't carry it. God sent these people to show me that Jesus will walk with me and lighten my load.

Secret number four: Being a Lone Ranger Christian is not what He planned for you. Sometimes people go to a church and just don't fit in. In other instances, people attend a church for a long time, situations go awry and lead to unresolved issues. Many circumstances surface that cause people to leave a church.

If this happens to you, lift your search up to Jesus, and systematically find the new church that He directs you to. Take your time. Do some research and try several different ones before you decide. I have known many families that have had a bad experience and never go back to church again. If this happens, the enemy has stolen the richness of life.

Secret number five: You guessed it! John 15:5. He loves you so much He suffered and died for you. Don't be afraid to talk to Jesus about absolutely anything, and remember: it's OK to ask and ask and ask. Luke 11:9-10 says, "And I tell you, ask, and it will be given to you; seek, and you will find; knock, and it will be opened to you. For every one who asks receives, and he who seeks finds, and to him who knocks it will be opened."

Secret number six: Just as going several days without food will cause you to become physically weak; going several days without reading the Bible will cause you to become spiritually weak.

Secret number seven: It is good to know where your money comes from. Deuteronomy 8:17-18 states, "Beware lest you say in your heart, 'My power and the might of my hand have gotten me this wealth.' You shall remember the Lord your God, for it is he who gives you power to get wealth; that he may conform his covenant which he swore to your fathers, as at this day."

Secret number eight: You who are saved have been chosen through the mercy of God, and you have been grafted. May it please God to bless you with inspiring knowledge that uncovers a mystery of the ages as you study chapters nine, ten, and eleven in the book of Romans.

To me these chapters are so exciting I can't sit still. Men walk the earth and ask why. Unfortunately, only those who are filled with the Holy Spirit can understand these chapters, and know why. Just as Colossians 1:15-20 explains that Jesus is the Meaning of the Universe, Romans 9, 10, and 11 explain this precious gift you have been given, why you will live forever, and why you will not be put to shame. Because you are going to study them I will just put in a couple of verses.

Romans 9:30-33 states, "What shall we say, then? That Gentiles who did not pursue righteousness have attained it, that is, righteousness through faith; but that Israel who pursued the righteousness which is based on law did not succeed in fulfilling that law. Why? Because they did not pursue it through faith, but as if it were based on works. They have stumbled over the stumbling-stone, as it is written,

> "Behold I am laying in Zion a stone
> that will make men stumble, a
> rock that will make them fall;
> and he who believes in Him
> will not be put to shame."

Now take a look at Romans 11:11-12, which states, "So I ask, have they stumbled so as to fall? By no means! But through their trespass salvation has come to the Gentiles, so as to make Israel jealous. Now their trespass means riches for the world, and if their failure means riches for the Gentiles, how much more will their full inclusion mean!"

Romans 11:19-20 tells us, "You will say 'Branches were broken off so that I might be grafted in.' That is true. They were broken off because of their unbelief, but you stand fast only through faith. So do not become proud, but stand in awe."

What makes these chapters the most exciting is the fact that God planned all this before time began in order to give glory to His First Born.

Secret number nine: Be careful if you get angry. The devil can use this anger as a weapon against you with skill and evil intent. Learn to give it to Jesus.

Secret number ten: Sharing your faith with someone is much easier than you might think. Spend one minute explaining that you were once a sinner. Spend two minutes telling of how you came to accept Jesus as your personal Lord and Savior, and take three minutes of your time to give an account of what it is like to live on earth and walk with Him, and live in His ways.

Secret number eleven: Live in a proven pattern of success. The people that God has used for His work in the Bible, and the people He has used since it was written have succeeded by living in the same pattern.

If you look at the lives of Abraham, Joseph, Moses, Joshua, Samuel, David, Isaiah, Jeremiah, Paul, Peter, Saint Augustine, or Saint Francis of Assisi, John Wesley, D.L. Moody, C.H. Spurgeon, Kathryn Kuhlman, Amy Semple McPherson, and so on, you will see the same pattern.

From their examples we see that:

- They were joined to God, their Father with a whole heart.
- They understood the job that they were chosen for and made it the number one priority in life. They were determined to do their best, all the while reverently respecting and submitting to His holiness.
- When worldly human desires or shortcomings distracted them, they asked for forgiveness and got back on track.
- They lived in the faith that they were given by Jesus to do their job. You would ask, "Did Jesus give Abraham and David and the other Old Testament people faith?" I would reply, "I think so."
- Their prayer life was honest, constant, and a key ingredient to success.

Here are my thoughts of each of these examples.

First: Each of these people had an awakening experience with God that connected them to Him forever, which was followed by a lifetime of deepening their relationship and obedience to Him. They served Him with an undivided heart.

Second: Their commitment was that of a willing servant. They learned to listen to Him with their mind and heart so as to correctly discern His will for their lives and daily walk in His ways with dedication, in order to complete the tasks given. Fear of God was instilled in each of their beings. They understood that God is so far above us that His holiness means that He is separate and distinct, and should be regarded with a higher respect and awe than any other consideration. Holiness is not an attribute of His character such as His loving nature, grace, mercy, knowledge and so on. Holiness is supremely who He is. In Isaiah 6:3 we read one of the most powerful statements in the Bible, "Holy, holy, holy is the Lord of hosts."

When we read a prayer from another on our list we see an understanding of God's supremacy. In Psalm 86: 8-13, David shows his reverence, knowledge of holiness, and love as he talks to His Father stating, "There is none like thee among the gods, O Lord, nor are there any works like thine. All the nations thou hast made shall come and bow down before thee, O Lord, and shall glorify thy name. For thou art great and doest wondrous things, thou alone art God. Teach me thy way, O Lord, that I may walk in thy truth; unite my heart to fear thy name. I give thanks to thee, O Lord my God, with my whole heart, and I will glorify thy name forever. For great is thy steadfast love toward me; thou hast delivered my soul from the depths of Sheol." Please read the passage again and notice how the back-and-forth child to Father love flows. David loves God and accepts His Father's love back into his spirit. Please read it a third time and notice how open and transparent the love, adoration, and exaltation David has for his Father. These words came from the deepest part of his soul.

Third: They repented and turned from their sins. While we live on this earth our sanctification is incomplete. We must strive for perfection, but the enemy of our soul keeps attacking us with temptations and accusations. Sometimes in our human weakness we fall astray. Of the people I have listed above two had noted scandals. The rest, I'm sure fought the desires and fears of this world constantly, sometimes getting in situations they regretted. The two that are famous for going astray are of course King David and Amy Semple McPherson. Both confessed, repented, and got back on track. Amy however, is surrounded by mystery and doubt because it is possible that she fully confessed to God, but may not have totally come clean to the public. We will never know. Having said that, I urge you not to discount her ministry because of the scandal. That would be a mistake. Her ministry was miraculous because she was chosen, she obeyed, and God was exalted. Studying her ministry would give you a new insight into the Power of God. She believed very strongly that God never changes, and spoke often about Hebrews 13:8, which truly tells us, "Jesus Christ is the same yesterday and today and for ever."

Fourth: Let us direct our attention to **faith**. Faith is often misunderstood. These successful people I have listed and many like them lived in their faith because of the type of close, personal relationship they had with God. It would have been impossible for any of them to do their jobs without the back-and-forth communication, and expectation—the aspect of faith that leads to success, and trust they needed to accomplish mighty things. I plead with Jesus each day for more faith so I can do my job better. Such behavior will put you through more trials, but He will answer your prayers. He is more interested in your character and trust in Him than He is your comfort. Rest assured, that at the end of the trials is Victory in Jesus! Your personal experiences as you walk in Christ will lead you to have the expectation of success that I previously talked about, thus leading to righteous confidence in your life. The greatest Power that exists walks with you. It's all about Jesus.

When Evelyn and I were newlyweds she went with me as I constantly visited as many Christian functions as I could. Three or four months went happily by and then it happened...the first derogatory remark. One evening in the car on the way home from a church supper, she voiced that she was unhappy with my response when people asked me what my religion was. Back then I always stated that I was a Kuhlmanite. She said that I almost made it sound like I worshipped Kathryn Kuhlman. For many years after her comment, I answered differently, usually telling people the name of the current denomination that God had instructed me to attend with my family. I now give a two-fold answer. I state the denomination of our home church and add that my religion is the church of the 'Kind.' I give an explanation that I visit Bible-believing churches of many denominations, whose members' lives revolve around Jesus, and in doing so I have uncovered a vastness of kind souls.

Having said that I would encourage you to study the ministry of Kathryn Kuhlman. She had a way of simplifying everything, and could explain how we can live in a faith that affects every area of our lives in a positive way. She spoke and wrote about being born again. She spoke of the rewards on earth and in heaven of working hard, loving your family, loving mankind, and having a Father-child relationship with Almighty God, and trusting in Him. She knew Jesus and reading about her relationship with Him is something you don't want to miss. There are many books written by and about her. "I Believe In Miracles" by Kathryn Kuhlman, and "A Glimpse into Glory" by Kathryn Kuhlman with Jamie Buckingham are, in my opinion, the two to start with. Reading them will also give you great Truths about the Holy Spirit and will fill your walk with knowledge.

Fifth: Talk to Him with your heart. He is more understanding than the human mind can imagine. Approach His throne of grace with reverence and honesty, and don't hold back your feelings. He wants to have a close relationship with you that will grow and last forever, and most of all He wants you to trust Him. This type of transparent relationship will help protect you from pride.

The more you learn to surrender your will and your time and thoughts to Him...the better it gets. When you truly are born again and have contact with Almighty God from within your heart, it is inevitable that living on this planet will change as you begin to see things through His perspective. As a soul in His Kingdom, you are gradually being given knowledge from a different spiritual dimension than those who live around you. They are trapped in the fallen dimension. Please don't get frustrated when communication breaks down between you and those in the fallen dimension. You used to live in it and stubbornly resisted God's righteousness before you were saved. The more you allow Jesus to be your Master—the more compassion you will have for lost souls.

Sanctification will bring more Jesus into you. Negativity will gradually be replaced with a more positive outlook. The devil will still tempt you with feelings of being a victim, a desire to blame others for your problems, a self-serving attitude, and a propensity toward self-pity; but you can now be aware of your enemy's tactics. When you lift each situation up to God and trust Him you will learn to walk in Christ, serve God and man, and have victory!

(Note...Beware. Let's take a minute or two and examine the opposite behavior—a mindset that I predict will result in being swallowed up by the evil one.) In today's world I have personally witnessed what I believe is false doctrine. I love people and have interviewed and kept in touch with numerous ministers in many Christian church denominations. Please study 2nd Peter 2. 2nd Peter 2:9-10 warns, "Then the Lord knows how to rescue the godly from trial, and to keep the unrighteous under punishment until the day of judgment, and especially those who indulge in the lust of defiling passion and despise authority."

In my opinion some who claim to represent Christ as His ministers have been given over and devoured by the enemy of their souls. Tricked into thinking that they can change the meaning of the Word to justify their [self] lusts and pride, they have adopted a behavior that is a direct assault on God's holiness. Their attitude and actions attack the righteousness that they claim to represent. It is most unfortunate that they are trapped in the fallen dimension and are unable to grasp the Spiritual journey and knowledge of the Bible that is given to those with an undivided heart.

I have listened attentively to many of these church leaders in private interviews. They sadly refuse to humble themselves and seek the Truth, the person Christ Jesus, and have a transparent relationship with Him. The people I am talking about are stubbornly unwilling to surrender their will and serve Him with a born again, whole heart. They don't believe in the Bible as it was written and are often identified by their pride, self-exalting wisdom, and/or denial of sexually immoral behavior as it relates to being a sin. They don't realize that in doing so they elevate themselves to the status of god; thereby denying that Christ's death on the Cross atoned for such sins.

Therefore, they are not justified by faith but are left drowning in their pride. I love these people but do not dare to remain in their proximity when lightning is around.

Please read Hebrews 4:12-16 which says, "For the word of God is living and active, sharper than any two-edged sword, piercing to the division of soul and spirit, of joints and marrow, and discerning the thoughts and intentions of the heart. And before him no creature is hidden, but all are open and laid bare to the eyes of him with whom we have to do.

Since we have a great high priest who has passed through the heavens, Jesus, the Son of God, let us hold fast our confession. For we have not a high priest who is unable to sympathize with our weaknesses, but one who in every respect has been tempted as we are, yet without sinning. Let us then with confidence draw near to the throne of grace, that we may receive mercy and find grace to help in time of need."

Secret number twelve: Walk in Power. It was one of those crisp fall days in New England. I rushed through traffic to get to an appointment on time. A pastor had discretely called me and asked me to drop by for a talk. Perhaps I could give him an idea or two about evangelism. The size of his congregation had remained about the same for a long time and no new converts had entered the Kingdom through his church. Back then a lot of Christians referred to me as an evangelist because I carried a Bible and pockets full of tracts most of the time. Sometimes I would get puffed up with pride and haughtiness when giving an account in church of how I had recently led someone to the Lord. I have repented. It's okay to recount instances of how souls are delivered from the evil one, but you must be careful to give all glory to your Savior.

Back to the story. I pulled into the parking lot just on time, straightened my tie, grabbed my briefcase, and ran up the steps and into the foyer. The pastor greeted me with a smile and an outstretched hand. We walked into his office and as we sat down, I pulled a notepad from my briefcase. We joked about the cool, comfortable nights and how the raw cold of winter was right around the corner.

I asked him what he had in mind for long-term goals and what he currently was doing regarding evangelism. Sadly, I listened and was not surprised as he gave me a complete description of the church body he was trying to create. He knew exactly how many parishioners he wanted, how 'holy' he wanted to teach them to be, and how he would manage his ideal flock of 'Mature Christians.' He had thought about and planned in detail every function inside a church. He was trying to move his church forward using a five-point plan. Evangelism was in the plan, but the church had been deeply involved in the other four areas and hadn't addressed it yet. He made no mention of any plans to minister to the poor and needy.

God had not, at that time, supplied me with knowledge to truly understand and help solve this pastor's problem. He was the third pastor I had talked to in an eight- or ten-month time period that I now believe needed more Power in his walk. I didn't know that then. The Lord has since equipped me with knowledge to identify and help pastors and others with this problem, and get them on a track of growth in the Great Commission.

I urged him to start small groups and home visits, and supplied him with a complete description of how to do so. We prayed and I left. Some time later, I learned that he had left the ministry as did one of the others that I mentioned.

Please understand. The man had Power, just not enough. The secrets of true, holy success are not easy to execute because of the struggle in our human reasoning. We hide pride and fear in little pockets in our minds and deny that they are there. A dichotomy exists in our thinking when we say to the world and ourselves that we want to surrender to God and walk in His ways, but pick and choose only the ways that feel comfortable. Forgiveness and witnessing Christ go against human nature.

There is a simple formula that is hard for us to follow because we embrace it with our mouths but fall short with our hearts and minds. Here is the formula: True Power comes from true holiness. **True holiness** comes from the Holy Spirit, walks in all of God's ways, shines like a light to the world, and glorifies Jesus.

Mature Christians are always trying to move forward by getting involved in outreach and making disciples. Each progressive stage of their sanctification brings a new phase of spiritual awareness into their life, which compels them to share with others and mentor those who God gives to them. They have Power in their lives and in their witness. Please read 1st Corinthians 4:14-21.

In the Bible I find a continual account of God's plan to rescue man, teach about the Kingdom of God, and glorify Jesus. It takes Holy Spirit Power to maintain focus in the Great Commission. Mark 1:14 teaches us followers, " 'The time is fulfilled, and the kingdom of God is at hand; repent, and believe in the gospel.' " Mark 1:17 teaches us, "And Jesus said to them, 'Follow me and I will make you become fishers of men.' "

In management school we were taught that there exists a management technique that is called 'Management by Lid.' Many businesses grow only to a certain point because the boss is thwarted by his or her self-known limitations, but they don't want to be exposed in their weaknesses. They intentionally and sometimes subconsciously 'put a Lid on it.' Many hard-working, talented people find it very frustrating to work in such an environment. In a church, those that end up staying under such leadership usually become very loyal but judgmental of outsiders, and critical of any slight variation in doctrine from what they have been taught. I call this the 'Fear Trap' because they are so contained they can neither hear God's voice nor equip the flock for true love—His way. We all have to watch out for this in our lives and churches. Jesus can free anyone from the traps I have mentioned when the problem is given to Him totally.

Somewhere in this book I typed out the Biblical passage that stated that Moses was the most humble person on earth. He always let it be known that he was walking in God's ways and not his own. He purposely wanted no glory for what he did. He worked, worshipped, adored, honored, respected, feared, and gave **all** glory to his Master Almighty God. Failure to break this pride-fear barrier of humanness has always been, and will always be, a large obstacle in outreach and unity. At one time or another, it affects all of us and all churches.

It is our very nature as Christians to humbly serve the poor and needy. Luke 14:11-14 tells us, " 'For every one who exalts himself will be humbled, and he who humbles himself will be exalted.'

He said also to the man who had invited him, 'When you give a dinner or a banquet, do not invite your friends or your brothers or your kinsmen or rich neighbors, lest they also invite you in return, and you be repaid. But when you give a feast, invite the poor, the maimed, the lame, the blind, and you will be blessed, because they cannot repay you. You will be repaid at the resurrection of the just.' "

In the Bible Jesus clearly tells us that it is our job as His Bride to reach out to the lost. We are the light of the world, not to be hidden under a basket. Jesus has been fully God forever, and brings holiness into our beings. The Father is a person and is the head of everything. Jesus is a person and your Savior and Master. The Holy Spirit is a person and also God as He is the third person in the Trinity. It is the Holy Spirit's Power that Jesus walked in while He was here in the flesh.

Let Jesus direct your thoughts and plans and invite Him into your daydreams. This can only happen if you really surrender and lift up all of your pride and fear. He is Holy and He will bless you with incredible Power, the Holy Spirit, to witness and do your job if you exchange your will for His. The Holy Spirit will make you a witness and a valuable soldier in the War. More Jesus equals more holiness (separated for God's purposes) and more Power in your life. Walk in Power, walk in Christ.

Read Isaiah 57:15 which tells us, "For thus says the high and lofty One who inhabits eternity, whose name is Holy: 'I dwell in the high and holy place, and also with him who is of a contrite and humble spirit.'"

Secret number thirteen: Don't be afraid of the number thirteen... or any other thing that causes unwarranted fear. God compels us to trust Him and tells us three hundred sixty-six times in the Bible to fear not. Satan wants you to be miserable and will tempt you constantly with fears. You must decide to reject them or be ruled by them. Fear can render you useless in the War. I believe that God's word teaches us over and over again that we should not focus on getting fear out as much as we should focus on getting Jesus *in*. Trust Him to take care of your fears. Walk in Power, walk in Christ. Please notice the words 'in' and 'peace' as you read the following passage. Philippians 4:6-7 tells us, "Have no anxiety about anything, but in everything by prayer and supplication with thanksgiving let your requests be made known to God. And the peace of God, which passes all understanding, will keep your hearts and your minds in Christ Jesus."

Secret number fourteen: God puts a helmet on women and sends them off to War. I love fundamentalist churches because they believe in every word of the Bible. I love to attend their services, hang around with them, work on feeding the poor in cities with them, work on missions with them, and study the Bible with them. I have spent hours enjoying fellowship, meals, and joking about thumping pages in the Bible with a lot of people, now close to me, who are fundamentalists.

However, I have recently learned that a small portion of the male leaders in them don't just thump the pages, they get upset when women in other Bible-believing denominations take an active role in speaking and teaching. When they get upset it wears me out. This is the second edition of this book. I was blasted after the first edition because I talked about women in ministry. I had no idea they would take such a strong stance and get angry.

Please let me explain. One of the first things I did when we cracked open the cases of books from the printer was to get copies into the hands of many friends who are fundamentalist leaders and parishioners. I was excited because I thought that my entire book verified their beliefs. After a few weeks I realized that there was only silence coming from that whole crowd. Then I made it a point to start asking several of them about how they liked the book. That led to an on-going flood of comments. They liked the book except…I needed to reprint it and take out any reference to women in ministry. When I tried to defend 'women in ministry' I got blasted and quickly dismissed.

The other day I was told that I continually sin because I like to watch Joyce Meyer on TV, and talk [out loud] about her teachings; and furthermore she sins because she teaches men. I was polite and bit my tongue. The same guys that pull me aside and now tear into me about this issue are too afraid to study the ministry of soldier Kathryn Kuhlman or soldier Joyce Meyer. They refuse to see how these women emptied themselves as vessels to be used by God. These guys have evidently not been exposed to the miracles surrounding the glory [given to Jesus] of ministries whose mission is to lift up the Son of God, and who have effectively led thousands and thousands of lost souls into the Kingdom. It is my opinion, after studying Ms. Kuhlman's ministry off and on for over twenty-eight years, that she was the most humble person on earth when she was ministering. She had power in her walk.

A few months ago I had a private visit with the pastor of an old New England church. I requested the appointment because his church was not growing and because of his reputation of running a controlled church. I wanted to honestly and tactfully ask him if we could discuss issues such as women in ministry, inviting less than perfect people into a flock, and variety of other subjects that bothered me. My motive was to see if a pastor with his mind-set would let me work with him and learn to reach into his community with God's love.

I had to walk up a couple of long, narrow, well-worn wooden staircases to get to his office. After a peaceful greeting I began discussing some of these issues. He abruptly ended the meeting and quickly walked out of the room. He is a big man. The whole place shook and creaked. It all happened so fast I didn't even get to the part about telling him that Kathryn Kuhlman often stated that she believed a woman should never be the leader of a church, and she backed her statements with sound scripture. It was a sad experience for me. He seemed to dismiss my work as being ridiculous. In my opinion he will probably live out his entire life without understanding that he missed huge blessings our God had planned for his ministry.

Please study Matthew 28:1-10, Mark 16:1-11, and Luke 24:1-11. You will see that God used women to announce to the world that Christ is risen from the dead. They were quickly sent to tell the Good News to Jesus' disciples. Do you really think they stopped talking after they told the disciples? As always, God knew the best way to get the job done.

If you read 1st Timothy 2:11-14 you will see plainly that Paul is addressing the authority a man should have over his wife in marriage. He goes directly to Adam and Eve as an example. A wife should never belittle her husband. Paul is also adamant about this in 1st Corinthians 14:33-35. In the Temple husbands sat up front with the men and wives sat in the balcony with the women. Many modern scientific studies conclude that men speak an average of five thousand words a day, and women twenty-five thousand...nothing has changed. There is to be order in worship, without the embarrassment caused by a wife disrupting the service by yelling at her husband. That doesn't mean that women can't speak in church. That doesn't mean that women can't teach. Paul gives us more details about this in Ephesians 5.

Let's take a look at Joel 2:28 which teaches us, "And it shall come to pass afterward, that I will pour out my spirit on all flesh; your sons and your daughters shall prophesy, your old men shall dream dreams, and your young men shall see visions. Even upon the menservants and maidservants in those days, I will pour out my spirit." We see in these words of God that women are to prophesy, which means 'to give instruction in religious matters.' We can clearly understand that these women must be filled with the Holy Spirit in order to do this.

Please go with me now to Acts 21:8-9, which is an account of the saints living in these same last days that Joel talked about and that we live in today. Luke and Paul visited the home of Philip the evangelist. We see that Joel's prophecy was beginning to be fulfilled. Philip's daughters were preachers of God's calling. They wore the helmet of salvation and were teachers. Philip's daughters were early soldiers in the War in which we fight for souls—the Great Commission. Please note that Paul didn't get upset about the women's teaching ministry. He and Luke stayed there for several days. Paul was very outspoken and had excelled as a Pharisee (see Acts 23:6 or Acts 26:5-11) because of his deep knowledge of scripture. He obviously felt comfortable with women teaching or we certainly would have heard about it.

Our text, "On the morrow we departed and came to Caesare'a; and we entered the house of Philip the evangelist, who was one of the seven, and stayed with him. And he had four unmarried daughters, who prophesied. While we were staying for some days, a prophet named Ag'abus came down from Judea."

Secret number fifteen: I have learned to hear His voice and you can too. When I was seven years old we lived in Camden, Maine quite far from town in an area of woods and fields. My older brother Bob had a few close friends his age, but there were usually no kids around my age that I could play with. I was allowed to go a certain distance from the house into the woods to a clearing. I would make my way to the clearing each day that the weather was good and sat perched on a large granite rock. The smells, sights, and sounds were exciting and constantly changing. Sitting very still was the goal, sometimes for an hour or more. One day everything seemed to come to a halt and it was almost like the sun was illuminating the clearing a little brighter. I suddenly had knowledge that God was real and He had created all of this.

Several times when I was an active evangelist, I would feel 'Tuned Up.' I would instantly have knowledge of a happening that would lead to someone's salvation. For instance, one day I was returning from a business meeting in Sanford, Maine and was on my way to Rochester, New Hampshire. It was mid-week in the middle of the afternoon and there was very little traffic. As I rounded a curve and went down the incline, I had instant knowledge of instructions. I was to pull over, and clear the junk off the passenger seat, and get a tract and a Bible ready. I pulled the car onto the shoulder of the road, and threw a couple of folders, and some paper work into the backseat, and grabbed a tract and a Bible. I knew with knowledge that could only come from God, that on the other side of the next big hill and then half way around the long curve that followed, there would a hitch-hiker. I was to pick him up, tell him my testimony, explain the salvation story, and lead him in the sinner's prayer.

Back on the road I went. Up and down the big hill and then about half way around the long curve...there he was. I pulled over and as he started to sit down in the passenger seat I said, "I'm Pete. I work for God." After he told me his name, I gave him my testimony of what life was like before I was saved, my conversion experience, and the peace and satisfaction of serving God as a Spirit-filled Christian. He accepted Jesus with his whole heart. I gave him the tract and dropped him off in Rochester by a church, and he promised to go to the church on Sunday.

For many years I had known when God was urging me to do something. To me, the experience of communication I described on the day of the hitch-hiker went far beyond urging, it was the voice of God. I did not hear an audible voice. I heard knowledge. Ms.

Kuhlman said repeatedly that she never heard an audible voice, but she absolutely knew when God was speaking to her.

I had asked my friend Kevin Hardy to co-author this book. I typed up the first four pages of my part, including an explanation of Baptism, addressed the envelope, and headed to the Post Office. I wanted him to have an idea of the type of material I had in mind in writing about individual involvement, and solving the mystery of how to successfully fulfill the Great Commission. On the way God spoke to me. In the description of Baptism he kept saying that I should rewrite it and include that part of Baptism is to "Spiritually Seal." I heard those words over and over. I had, at that time, never heard about this effect of Baptism or remembered reading it in the Bible. I went home, rewrote the page and mailed it to Kevin. Three days later I was reading Wesley and discovered that he talked extensively about this spiritual sealing. (By the way, Kevin had a full plate, and could not fit in time to write.)

"NOTHING!" God dictated a renewed path for the direction of this book with that and subsequent words. It was knowledge given instantly and loudly (but not audibly). Please note that until recently, each time the Lord has spoken to me, except when I was seven, involved vital knowledge that I needed to accomplish my job. I have since learned to be still in times of distress. There have been many instances where I have heard the voice of Jesus giving me peace and comfort as I lay my burdens before Him.

John 10:27 tells us, "My sheep hear my voice, and I know them, and they follow me."

Secret number sixteen: Let God fill the offering plate. The past ten years have included many serious discussions with various ministers struggling to make the church budget. I have studied and prayed about this and keep coming back to two basic reasons for success in having an overflow of money that comes into the church. They go hand-in-hand.

Reason one. Forget yourself and worship God. Is your church service a joyous celebration of God, so filled with love that flows back-and-forth between each person and God that it motivates your people? Without being urged, do they invite friends, co-workers, neighbors, family members, and others to church and to their small group? Is your service so filled with the Father's Love that it is the most fun in town?

Reason two. Serve the needy around you. Luke 6:38 states, "give, and it will be given to you..." Are the majority of your parishioners born again and walk in the Son? Do most of your people constantly witness Christ, know their gifts and serve in their chosen job, belong to a home group, are part of outreach, and read the Bible everyday?

Jesus never had billboards or brought attention to Himself by lifting Himself up. It was the Power in the work of the Father that He was doing that drew people, the touch of our Father's love. Members of your community will be drawn by the work of Jesus' kind of people that go and touch with the love of the Father.

Secret number seventeen: Live in the Word. It takes a while to get to a point where the Bible is your favorite book and you can't keep your hands off it. Seek wisdom about the Kingdom from the One who gives and gives to those who ask in the freedom of Christ. Let your walk in Christ be alive and refreshing as He leads you in daily reading.

Foursquare journaling is the best method of discovering the Truth that I have found when considering daily reading. I would like to recommend that you spend your first year living in an easy-to-read version of the Bible, and perhaps one with references.

I chose the Revised Standard Version for text references in this book for several reasons. It is very accurate, the syntax is from a slightly earlier time and hopefully causes you to stop and think through the points I'm trying to make, and it was my mother's Bible.

In my opinion your household budget should include saving for a new Bible each year, but please keep in mind that the accuracy of translation is important.

The following is a list of versions of the Bible that have been written with the accuracy of translation as a constant guidepost. They are arranged in order of closeness to word for word translation. I believe that all on the list fall within the boundaries of good Bible translations, but the ones closer to the end are written more in the style of thought by thought, and are not quite as accurate, but are easier to read. I used the Zondervan Bible Comparison Guide to make the list, which I obtained from my local Bible book store.

The List: Interlinear (word for word), New American Standard Bible, Amplified Bible, English Standard Version, Revised Standard Version, King James Version, New King James Version, Holman Christian Standard Bible, New Revised Standard Version, New International Version, Today's New International Version, New Century Version, New Living Translation, Contemporary English Version, and the New International Reader's Version (children ages 10 and under).

If you are new to reading the Bible, I suggest that you begin by simultaneously reading the books of John and Genesis. Then move on to Colossians, 1st John, and Exodus. Then search for a Foursquare journaling group or start one. I would like to note that a lot of churches have a three- to five-week class for new disciples that should give you an overview of the Bible.

Good News

When I was a kid I lived in a small community on the coast of Maine. There were many small farms dotting the countryside, a little bit of industry, and a whole lot of fishing. It sounds pretty fishy doesn't it? It was. It was great! A healthy percentage of the families that I grew up with were involved in fishing.

People were happy and actually walked down the street whistling. You could always spot a couple of guys leaning up against a pick-up truck, smiling and talking. There was the hustle and bustle of hard-working people, but it was seasoned with respect and happiness. You could hear laughter up and down the main street as women did their shopping. If you were bent over working you could hear the smiles without looking up. People worked hard all week and went to church on Sunday.

We kids had something called chores. We had to supplement the small amount of coins we received for odd jobs by walking along the roadside, and picking up soda bottles. Even that was fun.

Two things happened. At fourteen the devil took my hand. That was the one that rocked my life off kilter. The second thing was that electronics crept in. That was the one that rocked life in a small fishing village off kilter.

At first it seemed innocent enough. People started getting TV sets, and a leisurely hour or two was spent here and there watching a favorite show. Someone invented the fish finder. A few of the fishermen bought one. They caught so many fish, they bought bigger boats. The fish factories expanded, and hired more people. Money was flowing, and the pace of the whole town picked up a notch. People started desiring the extra things that they saw advertised on TV, and worked harder to get them.

Then, almost imperceptibly, life started getting a bit out of control. I didn't know that the devil was holding my hand. The town didn't know that an entity was skillfully edging in with negativity.

In school, you started hearing kids talking about how their fathers had to go further out to sea to catch fish. It was said that you couldn't even catch a haddock anywhere near the breakwater. Then the men bought more sophisticated electronics, and bigger boats, and went out even farther. It was assumed that all the activity drove the fish stocks into deeper waters.

The fog lifted. One fine beautiful day, complete with blue skies and fluffy white clouds, swooping gulls and girls on the beach, there it was. A giant Russian factory ship was anchored in front of our little paradise. It was far enough out to legally be there, but close enough to send a constant, gloomy message. Life as we had known it was gone forever.

A strange thing began happening to TV. The news gradually focused on more and more negative events in the world, and the shows painted a picture of more and more luxuries that somehow seemed to become essential.

Currently, the fish stocks are depleted so badly that they probably will never come back. The small farmers have almost completely disappeared. Most of the smiles are gone, and laughter is rare. TV is pumping out a two-fold, fine-tuned message of major negativity, and you've got to own more. Now on the street, you hear about a condition called depression.

Hold on. There is hope. Believe it or not, there are actually exciting, positive things going on in this world. Christianity is growing at a very fast pace. In fact, there is a global explosion in the growth of Christianity. Most surveys agree that currently, 2.3 billion people worldside identify themselves a Christian. That is approximately one third of the population of the earth, and the percentage of people that identify themselves as Christian is certainly increasing.

I tried to obtain accurate figures of how Americans identify themselves religiously speaking. The statistics regarding Christianity and Judaism were obtained from many recent polls conducted by different organizations, which all seemed to fall within the same range.

The other data is less certain as I averaged results from weeks of searching the Internet: Christianity 82% to 83%, Judaism 12% to 13%, and so on: Buddhism 0.5% to 0.8%, Islam 0.5% to 0.8%, Agnostic 0.5% to 0.8%, Atheist 0.5% to 0.8%, Hinduism 0.4% to 0.5%, Unitarian/Universal 0.3%, Wicca/Pagan/Druid 0.1%, Spiritualist 0.05%, Native American Religion 0.05%, Baha'i 0.04%, New Age 0.03%. These statistics may slightly change with the ebb and flow of culture, but the fact remains, you probably won't hear this on the news.

Airwaves, as you know, are controlled by the evil one. Breaking through this temporary (consult the book of Revelation) kingdom of the devil, requires surrender to God. While the news media and the entertainment business are busy with their high-profile, constant persecution of Christians, God is quietly winning.

I was blessed as God used the hands and heart of a friend to convince me to take the trip to Boston, and sit in a Fleet Center that was temporarily flowing with God's love. Our Father wanted me to hear His inspiring words as He spoke through Joel Osteen:

"He can make a way when there seems to be no way. The devil will try to discourage you and focus on bad things. Get in that attitude of faith. Don't dwell upon your problems. They draw negativity into your life. Turn your faith around, something good is going to happen today." He talked about Hebrews 11:1, which states, "Now faith is the assurance of things hoped for, the conviction of things not seen."

He also said, "God has us in the palm of His hand. Don't magnify your problems, do magnify your God! See yourself well. You'll never ride higher than the image you have of yourself. Don't listen to defeat. Listen to victory! I am blessed!" Then he quoted another scripture, Philippians 4:13, which tells us, "I can do all things in him who strengthens me."

When the crowd quieted down a little, he shouted, "I am a victor, not a victim! No weapon that is formed against me shall prosper!" He was referring to Isaiah 54:17.

He preached this powerful, positive message of hope for twenty minutes, and just when you thought it couldn't get any better he let us know that "God is a constant hope!" and referred to Jeremiah 29:11, which reads, "For I know the plans I have for you, says the Lord, plans for welfare and not for evil, to give you a future and a hope."

Then I was lifted out of my seat, "Get a vision! You are a child of the Most High God! Rise up and start acting like you have victory! Step up to the plate and deal with the things that are holding you back!"

The news media continually paints a negative picture of Christianity, and tries to pit us against each other. I sense they are trying to twist Mr. Osteen's message, and make it sound like he says that God wants us all to be rich. I didn't hear the man mention money. He did, however, have a salvation call.

I arrived home at midnight, and sat up until three thinking about all that had happened, and thanked the Lord for my friend who led me to such truth. It seems that the information about the event had been sent along with daily devotions that come from Joel Osteen via email. That's good news. There is even hope for electronics. To top it all off, he has a TV show!

Like This

Currently, I have embraced a challenge that involves spiritual warfare. Both of my support teams are helping in the fight, and I could use your help. Please pray. The battle is a matter of correct communication. Pastors hear about me, but don't get a full, accurate description of what I was sent to do.

There are a lot of growth consultants, growth programs, and books that are highly critical of pastors. I've seen too many anointed, hard-working, talented pastors become shamed. It is my opinion that these criticisms are unfair and undeserved. It is not my job to judge clergy in any way. They're the good guys.

God sent me here on planet earth to help clergy more effectively guide the process of how to change a church into a body that has full participation in the Great Commission. I try to work side-by-side with pastors, other leaders, and congregations to look at details and problems that need a fresh solution. If anything, it can be fun for the pastor, the other leaders, and the congregation as they form teams and move forward into the cycle of joy, peace, and love. I call it the 'most fun in town' when a church is focused on loving God, loving man, and making disciples.

There will be people in the church that will resist change. When you can get these very people involved in a work that uses their individual gifts as part of a unit of love, you will find that the resistance fades away and is replaced by a dedication to reaching the lost. They will start talking about what Jesus is doing in their lives.

Details

All of the above brings us to details that I like to discuss, one-on-one with leaders, to help begin the transformation process into a "Smiling Church." These details highlight priorities commonly found in "Smiling Churches."

In "Smiling Churches" there is constant prayer of surrender (John 15:5) to insure that the work performed is His. All leaders commit to daily Bible reading and encourage others to do the same. Witnessing is encouraged, especially in home groups. The majority of the congregation is involved in home groups. The poor, the lost, the hurting, and the incarcerated are talked about, planned about, prayed about, thought about, and ministered to. Israel is prayed for. Greeters greet and follow-up, ushers ush. The volume and quality of the sound is strictly and constantly monitored so it is absolutely perfect, not too loud or harsh, not too soft. The right type of lighting is used in each area of the church. There are two or more well-coordinated worship teams. There are easy-to-find signs for the restrooms. The length of the Sunday service usually runs between seventy and eighty minutes. The drama team highlights the pastor's message at least once a month, and well thought out video productions also can be a help. A friendly, well-marked parking lot with trained help for disabled people, an umbrella squad for rainy days, and special parking for first-time visitors are a must. All nursery workers are trained. The church constantly moves forward. The vision of the church is to impact the community with God's love. Sister churches in other areas are supported with prayer, finances, and visits. Watch out for wolves.

Just a Talk…

Pastors have often been reluctant to enlist my help publicly. That seems to be gradually changing. Recently, however, I was privately asked to give a step-by-step description of how an old New England church could get started on a path of growth. The average weekly attendance is approximately thirty-five souls, and fears of offending a mostly older congregation are a consideration.

I also recently met with a pastor privately, and he asked me to give him a step-by-step plan of how his congregation of approximately one hundred and fifty, on any given Sunday, could start growing.

To me, both situations involve the same set of procedures. Twice, when I was in training, I worked with churches that went from about twenty souls to well over two hundred, and continued to grow after I left. In my opinion, both churches will have the same type of spiritual battles to fight in order to get going, and then continue on. I recommend the following steps:

Step one: Wait on the Lord until you are at peace with moving forward. It takes two or more people to come to an agreement that your church should actively get involved in the Great Commission. This group, however large or small should first have a time of consultation with Jesus.

Step two: Survey all church leaders and any members of your flock that you feel have the gift of evangelism. Find out how they feel about your intentions to engage in active War and be on the offensive, and serve your community with a continuing outreach of love.

You must have united hearts committed to joining Him. All of your leaders must be in agreement about the church pursuing the Great Commission without reservation. All leaders must bring out their hidden scrolls, and get right with God. I strongly recommend including a good number of parishioners because leaders can't do this alone and you never want to cause the slightest rumble of 'us-against-them.' We are here on earth to work together, think together, and plan together, etc. You must achieve oneness of thought in order to have a church that successfully enters into and constantly moves forward in the Great Commission. Guiding each member of the church to consult Jesus with a transparent heart will drive out pride and lead to success.

At this stage, I recommend that each of the people involved read this book, and conduct a focus group study to expand your thinking about the future and how to incorporate the different skills within your flock.

Each step, of course has to be directed by prayer that is in agreement. John 15:5

Step three: Announce your plan to the congregation. Tell them that you will be visiting them in their homes to explain the details. Make this announcement in the middle of the service, and spend the rest of the service making appointments. In the case of the larger church, meet with small groups of individuals and families that live near each other. Yes, please have everyone read this book.

Step four: Put the plan into action. Everyone discovers their spiritual gifts, and is encouraged to use these gifts to serve Him in their chosen job. As the church grows, it is often helpful to form two or more teams for every task, not to compete with each other, but rather to support, complement, and encourage each other, and to share the load. For instance, in my new home church the small groups take turns cleaning the church. It is done efficiently and effectively each week, and each group follows a set order of procedures. The church is always cleaned in exactly the same way and is spotless. If you have thirty-five home groups, each will clean every thirty-fifth week.

Learn to identify and fight spiritual battles. Listen to Jesus and establish a plan for moving forward again as your congregation learns to work together as one unit of love. There will always be spiritual battles, so when it gets a little overwhelming please remember Psalm 91:1-2, which reads, "He who dwells in the shelter of the Most High, who abides in the shadow of the Almighty, will say to the Lord, 'My refuge and my fortress; my God, in whom I trust.'" You are not doing this by your own power.

Take time to work with those that have been given a gift of compassion for the poor and needy. A successful church needs this ministry, and part of your budget must be allocated for support.

Go through the list of details in this book. Cover everything in prayer. Train parking lot attendants, install first-time visitor parking signs, train greeters and ushers, and so on. Organize home groups, form strategy teams, and encourage everyone to share what the Lord is doing in their life. If you do not get a high percentage of participation at this stage you have more spiritual battles to fight.

Step five: Develop a humble, open, and flexible pair of praise and worship teams that can interact and exchange members. Psalm 98:1 states, "O sing to the Lord a new song, for he has done marvelous things! His right hand and his holy arm have gotten him victory." Ask the Lord to provide you with a leader that is right for the job of managing your music. You want the very best musicians in your area to be saved and merged into your worship as you lift your Lord in glory. Set up auditions on a regular basis. As the church grows, so will the level of professionalism, unity, and the number of musicians. At the same time, you should encourage others to join that have a heart for music, a desire to participate, and are eager to develop their skills.

In the music program overall, the Lord wants us to use the gifts he has given to these musicians to blend our hearts together, lifting Him in glory. Whether you are singing traditional hymns, modern day praise songs, or a mix, commune with your Maker from deep within.

Step six: Gently confront individuals who are not involved in outreach. Make it clear how to get involved. It has been my experience that sometimes talented, well-meaning souls are mistakenly left out and their feelings get hurt.

Step seven: Leadership committees should form teams to conduct special events. These events can be unique to your church, and can reach out to your community. Your church, and each individual within your church, is unique and gifted. Idea searching within the church can produce interesting results. Each phase of growth must be encouraged, and led by leaders' personal involvement. All of this might sound exhausting, but as the church grows, souls will rise up to fill leadership roles. God created each of us to enjoy serving Him in our own chosen way.

It is my experience that entering into and continually moving forward in the Great Commission happens in stages. Several churches that I have worked with have seemed to reach new victories, in getting people and activities in place, by building what I call a ramp of momentum, if you will, that allows them to spring into the next stage of outreach. To me each stage of this growth happens roughly in five- or six-month time periods. When you reach the eighteen-month mark it is time to have a major evaluation.

Learn to listen to Him as you serve and share. Go. Love God, love man, and make disciples! Your church will gradually become a "Smiling Church."

The Most Important Moment

God gave the Bible as a gift to humanity. In it, He reveals the Truth about who He is, and how we can choose to become His children. He also tells us all we need to know, right now, about His Kingdom, and how we can serve Him.

He shows us that He is not an uncaring God that watches us from a distance, but rather a loving God that cares about every detail of our lives. He wants to have a close personal relationship with each one of us. He shows us His likes and dislikes, tells us how to please Him, and tells us what He finds detestable.

The Lord goes to great length in the Bible to reveal His character, detailing the consequences of mocking Him, and the benefits of obeying His commands.

You owe it to yourself to learn about the One who created you, and all that is created. If you lift your entire being up to Him, and surrender ownership to Him by accepting His Son Jesus as your personal Lord and Savior, then you can read the Bible with guidance from the Holy Spirit. If you do that, you will fall in love with Him. This love will last forever.

John and Charles Wesley, Kathryn Kuhlman, Dave Adams, Doug Tunney, Peter and Lisa Bonnano, and all the others that I have listed in this book are just people that chose to read His Word and completely surrender to Him. He called each to a specific job and uniquely equipped each one with special gifts for their appointed task. They chose to obey. I encourage you to follow their lead.

After I had read the Bible for a couple of years, I began to see Jesus in passages that didn't mention Him. For instance, read the first chapter of John and the first chapter of Colossians, and you will see

Jesus in the first chapter of Genesis. After more years of reading, Jesus started to emerge constantly. I realized that He was illuminating each page for me, and the history of man became His story.

The most important moment in the history of mankind happened on the Cross when the **Son of God died in atonement for our sins.** The shed blood of our precious Lord paid the penalty for a lost world and offers forgiveness. Man's separation from God because of sin, can be overcome by accepting the Lamb of God who was sacrificed for us. God in His mercy has given us this choice. 1ˢᵗ John 3:8 states, "The reason the Son of God appeared was to destroy the works of the devil." We who are born again, and have elected to join Him in the Great Commission, the rescue of those who overcome, are in awe of the words that our Savior spoke in Luke 19:10 when He said, "For the Son of man came to seek and to save the lost." These words resonate in each of us even today.

If you are new to reading the Bible, I suggest that you ask a church leader to go over the following Bible references so you will have a better understanding of the Cross: Exodus 12, Isaiah 53, Romans 3:25, and Leviticus 17:11.

It was on the Cross, that the Lamb of God poured out His blood; blood so powerful that in a moment the final covenant was sealed between God and man. A couple of years ago I accompanied my friend Ron, a pastor, to hear several speakers in Boston. The most awe-inspiring message I have ever heard was when Almighty God spoke through Henry Blackaby. I couldn't tell you if he spoke for twenty minutes, or forty minutes, or sixty minutes. All I know is that we were captivated as we stood in the balcony and listened to him preach about the power of the Cross.

The grave is empty! God's plan for the redemption of man and glory to the Lamb all came together as Jesus suffered and died, and rose from the dead, and was highly exalted above all others. His Resurrection from the dead is one of the greatest proofs that Jesus is exactly who He said He was—the Son of God and the only One through whom eternal life is offered. Philippians 2:8-9 teaches, "And being found in human form he humbled himself and became obedient unto death, even death on a cross. Therefore God has highly exalted him and bestowed on him the name which is above every name, that a the name of Jesus every knee should bow, in heaven and on earth and under the earth, and every tongue confess that Jesus Christ is Lord, to the glory of God the Father."

Christ's resurrection completed the mystery of our salvation and redemption; by His death Jesus freed us from sin and by His Resurrection He restored to us the most important privilege lost by sin. Romans 4:22-25 shows us, "That is why his faith was 'reckoned to him as righteousness.' But the words, 'it was reckoned to him,' were written not for his sake alone, but for ours also. It will be reckoned to us who believe in him that raised from the dead Jesus our Lord, who was put to death for our trespasses and raised for our justification."

By His Resurrection we acknowledge Christ as the immortal God, the efficient and exemplary cause of our own resurrection. 1st Corinthians 15:20-21 tell us, "But in fact Christ has been raised from the dead, the first fruits of those who have fallen asleep. For as by a man came death, by a man has come also the resurrection of the dead." Jesus' Resurrection defeated death.

Now take a look at the wonderful new body we will receive on the other side of the grave because of the sacrifice of our precious Lord. Philippians 3:20-21 tells us, "But our commonwealth is in heaven, and from it we await a Savior, the Lord Jesus Christ, who will change our lowly body to be like his glorious body, by the power which enables him even to subject all things to himself."

The Bible is the living Word of God. Proof that all of this is true is available to any man or woman who will seek Him in earnest. (Please see details in the 'You Decide' section of this book.) If you are a surrendered soul that is born again He will come to live within your heart. Acts 2:32-33 states, "This Jesus God raised up, and of that we all are witnesses. Being therefore exalted at the right hand of God, and having received from the Father the promise of the Holy Spirit, he has poured out this which you see and hear."

It is our job to lead all of the lost souls that we can to Him to be saved. Look what happens to those poor souls who reject Him. Philippians 3:19 sadly teaches us, "Their end is destruction, their god is the belly, and they glory in their shame, with minds set on earthly things."

Together in Love

We who are saved are now aliens on earth as our citizenship is in heaven. 1ˢᵗ Peter 2:11 tells us, "Dear friends, I urge you, as aliens and strangers in the world to abstain from sinful desires, which war against the soul." The more you learn to surrender your will to Him, and trust Him, the easier it gets to live here on this planet. We are living in uncertain times, but rest assured, He is in charge.

1ˢᵗ Peter 2:5 states, "...and like living stones be yourself built into a spiritual house, to be a holy priesthood, to offer spiritual sacrifices acceptable to God through Jesus Christ."

It's time to let Him draw us together in unity. We are a holy nation and we are under attack.

1ˢᵗ Peter 2:9 states, "But you are a chosen race, a royal priesthood, a holy nation, God's own people, that you may declare the wonderful deeds of Him who called you out of darkness into His marvelous light. Once you were no people but now you are God's people; once you had not received mercy but now you have received mercy." Let's not be selfish with this free gift of mercy that we have received in our salvation. Rather, lift our lives up to Him as living sacrifices of praise so our church will love God, love man, and make disciples.

Smile

There are many reasons to smile. Playing with children, good grades in school, winning a game, a little comedy thrown into a sermon, reuniting with loved ones, and just plain being positive are but a handful of situations that cause us to smile. Unfortunately, we currently live in a world with two Kingdoms. One is light and of God, and one is dark and of the evil one.

When shadows come and things don't go as planned, we all experience bad times. My friend Kevin Hardy, Senior Pastor of a "Smiling Church" says, "You've got to have bounce."

Sometimes situations happen that are very hard to bear and to understand. It may take a considerable amount of time before you gradually heal from the sting of a tragedy. You may always remember the occurrence, but He wants to heal and restore you, and help you regain your joy in Christ. Your small group members are there to listen, love, pray, and help. It is extremely important as you learn to walk in victory that you cling to your Savior and His people when you are having a wilderness experience, all the while realizing that He is walking through this with you.

The other night I received sad news, and it took the wind out of my sails. I immediately called a home group member, Rick B., and then I called my dear friends Jerry and Jann in Tennessee. I was in a home group with them many years ago. Jerry and Jann have intermittently experienced sorrows, yet they usually seem joyful, laugh a lot, and have a deep compassion for others. I told them the details and asked them to pray. We talked for a long time, and somewhere in the conversation they told me that they had given absolutely everything to God, and they trust Him. Everything. You must forgive, give it to the Lord, walk with Him, and wait on Him. Then you can have bounce.

It took me years to learn that I always need to belong to a small (home) group, and it took me years to learn to trust Him to lift my spirit after suffering from life's woes. When time has passed and I'm ready, I try to get alone inside His word because I know He wants me to smile again. The following is a description of how I meditate in His Word. I'm sure that there are many ways to meditate, but this process works for me.

I sit in a comfortable position with good posture. Then focus on my breath. Genesis 2:7 states, "then the Lord God formed man of dust from the ground, and breathed into his nostrils the breath of life; and man became a living being." Learning to relax comes with time, but the three-part breath can be very beneficial. Gently breathe in air so as to first fill your lower abdomen, then the chest, and then the clavicle area. Fill it all with a good, slow, deep breath; and then release with a big whoosh. Do several of these deep breaths at your own pace, and relax.

Next, focus on the power of the Cross. This expresses God's love in its purest form. The blood of Christ was the ultimate sacrifice. Look at what our Savior said about His suffering. Luke 23:34 states, "Jesus said, 'Father forgive them; for they know not what they do.'" Go through cycles of normal and then deep breathing, and love as you forgive every person who has wronged you. Imitate your Savior. Each time you whoosh out and relax, propel the toxin of bitterness that has prevented you from forgiving, out with the air.

Now it is time to smile. Gently and gradually use your face muscles, and pull back the corner of the right side of your mouth, just a little bit. Then gently curl it up, just a little. Repeat this process on the left side. You should start feeling a pleasant sensation that starts in these two locations, and travels elsewhere in your body. I have been told that by doing this, a chemical is produced that makes us feel good.

You are now ready to meditate in His Word. Pick positive passages in the Bible that will help sustain your smile. Find testimonies in the

Psalms and other books that tell of our Lord's help, His protection, His power, His greatness, His love that endures forever, and His **strength** that is within you. Ephesians 3:16-17 states, "that according to the riches of his glory he may grant you to be strengthened through his Spirit in the inner man, and that Christ may dwell in your hearts through faith: that you, being rooted and grounded in love, may have power to comprehend with all the saints what is the breadth and length and height and depth, and to know the love of Christ which surpasses knowledge, that you may be filled with all the fullness of God." Please remember that He is able to heal and restore, if only you will let Him come in and love you. Look at how Paul ends that third chapter. Ephesians 3:20-21 states, "Now to him who by the power at work within us is able to do far more abundantly than all that we ask or think, to him be glory in the church and in Christ Jesus to all generations, for ever and ever. Amen." As I meditate in His Word, I am reminded that this isn't about me, it's about Him. He is in me, and I do what I do to glorify the Lamb. I'm part of Jesus' team, and we are defeating the devil by winning souls, so I rest in His love.

Because I live on the road a great deal of the time, I don't always have the opportunity to meditate. My long experience knowing and trusting Jesus, and seeing His faithfulness time after time has now elevated my faith to a level that brings a peace that amazes me. When I'm feeling down, or anxious, or sad, or insecure, or inadequate, or fearful, or alone, or guilty because I just pigged out on too much chocolate, I stop what I'm doing, and have a talk with Him. I give Him a detailed account of how I feel, and my version of how I got into this trying predicament. Then I trust Him with absolute surrender. "Jesus, this is all bigger than me. I don't want it. I give it all to you." Then I wait. A minute passes. I wait. Another minute passes. All of a sudden it happens. A big smile comes across my face! This smile didn't come from me, it came from Him! Everything will be alright.

Sent

Portions of the U.S. Gulf coast were devastated after Hurricane Katrina. Some communities chose to use the world news media to complain about unjust rebuilding efforts by the government. From my viewpoint many residents of communities in Mississippi used a different approach. What I saw from them was a natural pleading of people with faith in God, and a response from their Heavenly Father of power and love. He not only heard their cries for help, He sent an army of His people. He sent money and resources. He sent tools, and trucks, and food, and building materials from Christian churches all over the U.S. and Canada. Lest I not forget to mention, He sent Dan Lynch, Sandy Donnelly, Dave Epstein, Cheryl Outlaw, and me from Grace Capital Church in central New Hampshire.

The particular group that we served in was put together and managed by Beaverton Foursquare Church from Oregon, in conjunction with the Salvation Army, and several other charitable organizations. We were headquartered in a project center owned by the Salvation Army, as part of a team drawn from many Christian denominations. Each of us was amazed by the unity. The thought of denominations was immediately forgotten, and not part of the equation of love and friendship that increased each day we were there. Jesus was in charge. He saw where our Father was working, and sent His disciples to be the hands and hearts to carry out the work.

When we first arrived Saturday afternoon we busied ourselves with becoming familiar in our new surroundings, and enjoyed the orientation by the Beaverton management team. Sunday was our first full day, and we asked around to get directions to a near-by church. It pleased the Lord to bless us as we attended the New Bethel Missionary Baptist Church. We arrived a little early and sat in a pew off to the right side about two thirds of the way to the front. As the people filed in they all came over to greet us. They welcomed us with smiles, extended hands, and hearts that genuinely made us feel that we belonged there.

The Reverend Kenneth E. Hollins walked up to the lectern and opened the service by leading us all in praises and songs. The all-male singing group was incredible as they left their seats and moved up front to minister to us. Then Pastor Hollins preached a message of truth in a way that captured our attention every second he spoke. His vocal resonance, humor, subject knowledge, and anointing came from a filling of God rarely seen or heard. It was wonderful to say the least. He spoke from 1st Corinthians 13:4, which states, "Love is patient and kind." I believe his version said, "Love suffers long and kind." He said, "However long the Lord has us in circumstances, we endure hardness as good soldiers of Jesus Christ." He explained about Job's circumstances, and how he endured.

Pastor Hollins continued on and said, "Don't run from trouble. People don't want to go through anything. We want sunshine everyday. You won't appreciate the sun if you don't have rain." Then he compared hard times to going through a valley. "You have to go through the rich soil of the valley so you can appreciate the mountain. Trouble is in the valley. The topsoil and the fertilizer are in the valley. Every time we go through the valley we grow some." Then he talked about how we are to forgive. He said, "Get a long fuse." He told stories about his home life, and about old TV shows that were very funny, and he related them to having a short fuse, but thankfully his wife has a long fuse. We are to be patient and kind.

The pastor then leaned over the pulpit and spoke powerfully as he compelled us to understand more scripture that connected us to our God right now. He said, "2nd Peter 3:9 reminds us, 'Remember how the Lord suffers long waiting for us.' " Pastor Hollins instructed us to be willing to forgive, and he cited Mark 11:25-26, which says, "And whenever you stand praying, forgive, if you have anything against any one; so that your Father also who is in heaven may forgive you your trespasses." Then he talked about love. He urged us to "Love one another," which he quoted from 1st Peter 4:8. He stood back and raised his hands in the air, and cried out, "They nailed Love to a tree! Angels could have rescued Him, but He chose to suffer and die for us!" Every eye had a tear in it as he slowly shouted, "One Friday He laid it down, but Sunday morning He picked it up again!" Listening to this man preach was an experience we will never forget. There's more. He prayed. Oh, did he pray! "Lord, hold back the hand of death!" He talked to our Father about the situations of healing, and rebuilding, and of love that suffers long and is kind. Then as the people were humming 'Amazing Grace' he prayed, "Dear Lord, spring our eyes open so that we might behold the glory of Jesus!" I don't have the words to describe what a joy it was to hear this man preach, listen to all the wonderful singing, and feel loved.

Monday morning we started work. The work itself basically fit into a scenario of what each of us had expected, but that was the only thing that did. The genuine overflowing of warmth, love, and appreciation coming from everyone we met that had lived through the tragedy of the storm, and the aftermath that followed affected us more than we had ever imagined. We all had a preconceived notion of what we were going to do in Mississippi; help rebuild, and get to know a few people. We had no idea that we would fall in love. Time seemed to stop. You could feel God's presence everywhere. I have often read in 1st John 4:8 where the Word states that God is love, but I had never felt His love surround me like it did in Mississippi. I had never felt His strength as He was comforting His people, and filling them to overflowing with His love.

The Bible teaches us that the work we do here is eternal as we serve our God. I think that I really started to appreciate this eternal nature of work with each new resident I met. It wasn't just the smile and the handshake, but an initial connection with a family member that will continue on and last forever.

On the plane back to Boston God urged me to read and meditate on Psalm 95. I read it eight or nine times, and meditated on the text for an hour or two. I was pleasantly reminded that I enter His rest with peace and joy as my life is in Christ.

During the flight, our group leader, Dan Lynch, sat beside each of us for a while. He interviewed us about our impressions of our week in Mississippi from a series of questions he had previously prepared. He wanted spontaneous responses while the weeklong experience was fresh in our minds. Following are some of our thoughts:

1. What impressions did you have about this trip?

Sandy: I was impressed by the ability of the long-term volunteers to follow up with the homeowners, and people they worked with, and their overall organizational skills. Also, I was struck by how these volunteers loved to introduce new workers to the locals, and how excited they would get with each meeting.

Dave: God is orchestrating the whole thing from beginning to end. He planned who would go, and what they would do. It was His choice that placed each of us there. It all happened like it was supposed to.

Cheryl: How grateful, cheerful, and happy the people were. How God has turned this tragedy around.

Dan: I couldn't believe the scope of the devastation. It looked like an atomic bomb went off on the coast of southern Mississippi. Also, I couldn't believe the love and spirit of the locals...truly supernatural under the circumstances. I also couldn't believe the response of the body of Christ. The town is being rebuilt entirely by Christians. Knowing that so many hear Jesus' voice, and are willing to serve has become a huge encouragement to my feelings about fellow Christians.

Pete: He sent me to Mississippi to fall in love with people that were not wealthy in a financial sense, but were rich in God. All of the folks we met had lost a relative or a friend in the storm. I ended up having a great deal of respect for each of them, and will always be in awe of their faith in God.

2. What was the most memorable moment?

Sandy: Having lunch with the other workers. They were of different ages, denominations, skills, and backgrounds; but they were all excited to share what they were working on, and had a glow about them because they were serving God, and helping a community with His goodness.

Dave: Mentoring the young man that worked with me. I feel that teaching him was the main reason God sent me to Mississippi.

Cheryl: Being part of an organization with different faith-based groups working together, and not separated by denomination. That was impressive to me.

Dan: Interacting with the people who live there. I have never met more positive, thankful, gracious, and forward-looking people in my life, especially given the devastation to their own personal lives over the past sixteen months.

Pete: There were seven or eight memorable moments for me. All but one involved a private conversation with local people or coworkers, instantly achieving the same mindset, and a closeness that doesn't happen very often in life. The other moment was every detail involving the people in church, and the love that flowed in church. Church was great!

3. What did you take away from this trip?

Dave: An amazing increase in my desire to serve the Lord! What a blessing it is to give! This is a huge revelation given my prior life of wanting to pursue possessions. I also take away a sense of value in the gift that God is urging me to use to serve youth. I now have His confidence to move forward and serve.

Sandy: The need is still great in Mississippi. You want to

accomplish as much as you can in a short period of time because of the enormous need. I was also impressed by the gratitude of the homeowners, the neighborhood folks, the long-term volunteers, and all the church people.

Cheryl: People need to know that a lot of help is still needed in Mississippi. Our Lord wants His servants to be involved emotionally, spiritually, and physically. I also take away from this trip more confidence regarding my own spiritual growth and insight.

Dan: That we have so much and yet don't appreciate what we have; and people who aren't as comfortable seem to rely on God more than we do, and as a result, have a closer and more real relationship with God. They also seem to appreciate what little they have more. A lot more work has to be done. God will touch the hearts of Christians, and it will happen. I also take away from this trip a story to be told about Mississippi that the public has no idea about. Incredible work is being done, but you don't hear about it.

Pete: My ability to surrender took a giant step forward. God took over. The fear of God came into play when I realized the power of His presence. Also, Mississippi shows us all that there is no power that exists that compares with His. He heard the prayers of His people and answered with such a mighty response that it would be hard to believe unless I had seen it first hand.

Dan asked several other questions which unveiled common thoughts among us. We all were pleasantly surprised by the enjoyment of nightly journaling together. Sharing that specific group time of Bible reading and journal writing, and reading our daily journey in His Word out loud all became very comfortable.

The absolute sovereignty of God that gathered His workers to do this mighty work was another common thought, which changed all of our lives, and changed our perception of how omnipotent our

God is. We were exposed to the realm of His authority and unlimited power. One other long lasting impression amongst each of us was the peace and satisfaction that sustains when you serve God in a job that He chose for you. It's more than a feeling. It becomes part of your being just as living in Christ becomes part of your being.

Now that I am back in my office, I just received an email from one of my new friends who was a coworker in Mississippi. Louie is from Oregon. He humbly wrote of how privileged he feels to have been part of this great work of God.

Psalm 31

Psalm 31:1 states, "In thee do I seek refuge; let me never be put to shame." Here David talks to our Lord about the storms and troubles of this life, about the threat of enemies, and of eternal salvation. Verses three through five continue, "Yea thou art my rock and my fortress; for thy name's sake lead me and guide me, take me out of the net which is hidden for me, for thou art my refuge. Into thy hand I commit my spirit; thou hast redeemed, O Lord, faithful God."

David was pressed on all sides, yet did not panic, but rather surrendered all to God. Look at verse fifteen, **"My times are in thy hand."** (Please note: The bolding is mine because it is one of my favorite passages in the Bible. David doesn't know the outcome, but has absolute trust in God, and states clearly that all that he is and has is committed to his Father, now and forever.)

Today we are pressed from all sides. Christian persecution is beginning to gain momentum as the devil sets his pawns in place. We have a choice. We can panic, or we can choose to place our trust and times in our Father's hand. We can choose to forge onward, and to go and love in the capacity He has created each of us for.

A few weeks ago our church had a guest speaker. He talked about discovering and developing the job that God created us for. Each soul was created for an individual, unique purpose. The speaker said that we all have a dream factory deep inside. To find your job, invite Jesus into your dream factory and have Him show you who you really are.

Over the past twenty-nine years I have belonged to many home groups and visited many others. The one I am in now is only the third one out of all of them that has been run properly, and constantly moves forward. Our leader, Dianne, was chosen for the job before God laid the foundations of the earth.

The meeting opens with prayer and praise. I lead us in a couple of hymns. Dianne takes over for the rest of the meeting. She starts by going over each detail of the pastor's message that week, and each of us are asked to comment on how these details are involved in our lives. People are people, and many times will wander off the subject. Dianne is skillful, pleasant, and adds a little twist of humor as she interjects to refocus, and get us back on task.

This week a new lady, Beth, visited us for the first time. She is fun to listen to and blessed us with interesting insights during our discussion. I hope she becomes a regular member.

Outreach is then thoroughly discussed. Most of us are either involved in "going and loving," or participate in church activities or intercessory prayer, which supports our 'go and love' work. Others focus on receiving souls into the church, and loving, teaching, and supporting them as they are commissioned to work in their calling.

This group of love that I now belong to has a very active membership. Rick is a big man, but humbles himself as he ministers with selected members of other small groups and serves the homeless. He also sometimes travels far away to use his skills as a contractor, helping sister churches in other areas, as they carry on building projects to help the poor. Tammy is organizing packages, notes of love, and prayer for missionaries our church supports as they serve in sister churches in Africa, Russia, and Canada. Denise is an intercessor; Joan is involved with children's ministry; Tracy volunteers her time in our Café, is a crew leader on the church's cleaning crew, and in the summer, supervises at Teen Camp. Our other Tracy and Mattie are ushers. Belle also has a heart to serve by coordinating ministries in our elderly community. Sarah ministers to teens. Frank's surrendered heart leads him to ministering to many. He is always willing to lend a hand by helping with odd jobs.

Our group is then directed to prayer. A list is made, and several of us take turns praying for whoever is hurting or sick in our midst.

We also pray for each detail of the many outreaches, and for family, friends, coworkers, church leaders, our country, and a variety of personal requests.

The more I look around in this church, the more I'm amazed at the number of outreaches that affect our community with God's love. This church is moving forward. Though the storms of life surround, all is surrendered to serve and trust God.

It is my opinion that the teachings, actions, and love in a church like this lead to a quality of life that cannot be reached any other way on earth. Take for instance, the support of prayer and caring in a home group, or the teaching about how to recognize when the devil wants us to feel bad because he accuses us, and wants us to feel guilty about some small thing we said or did. Our senior pastor has taught us to be watchful of the enemy's ways, the 'runs' of the accuser as he tries to control us. Satan wants to rob us of our joy in life. John 10:10 tells us, "The thief comes only to steal and kill and destroy; I came that they may have life, and have it abundantly." Jesus offers us life in Him.

I have visited and monitored church after church after church, which appear to be directed by men. Most everything they do, apparently, is generated in the minds of men. They are of a religious nature, but the fire of God is missing. In my new home church, and other "Smiling Churches," people are on fire for God! None of this fire comes from them, but from God. This fire is only received through an act of total trust and surrender. Too many miss the point, and think they serve Him as they actually serve themselves in the flesh.

The first step to victory must always be the fear and respect of Almighty God. Leviticus 9:22 through 10:3 reads, "Then Aaron lifted up his hands toward the people and blessed them; and he came down from offering the sin offering and the burnt offering and the peace offerings. And Moses and Aaron went into the tent of meeting; and when they came out they blessed the people, and the glory of the Lord appeared to all the people. And fire came forth from before the Lord and consumed the burnt offering and the fat upon the altar; and when all the people saw it, they shouted, and fell on their faces.

Now Nadab and Abi'hu, the sons of Aaron, each took his censer, and put fire in it, and laid incense on it, and offered unholy fire before the Lord, such as he had not commanded them. And fire came forth from the presence of the Lord and devoured them, and they died before the Lord. Then Moses said to Aaron, 'This is what the Lord has said, 'I will show myself holy among those who are near me, and before all the people I will be glorified.' And Aaron held his peace."

Your time is valuable. Your life is valuable. Take refuge in your God. Let Him guide you, and be your rock, and your salvation. Serve Him with a fire that only He can give you.

I took an extra few months to pray and ask God for each word in this book. As I am now in the process of finishing up, I notice that this little church of ours has an average weekly attendance of over nine hundred.

More Than a Building

It has been said that the attitude of a man determines how far he will go in life. I believe that the same principle holds true for a church. It is the collective mindset, the attitude of victory in Jesus, the **attitude** of unity, and the **attitude** [of servants] to maintain a focus on God's will that determines how far a church will go in life, and how successfully it will blend with its community, and win souls for Christ. I think that all members of a church need to be aware of this parallel that equates success in a church and success in an individual. If examined, they will show us a pattern for victory.

Our battlefield is in the hearts and minds of people. The tactics of the enemy can be thwarted by simple awareness, open discussions, and by taking action against him. Our attitude is completely affected by our spirit. If we are not watchful, the enemy will slip in unnoticed, link negative thoughts to negative thoughts, and steal joy and positive direction from each of us. We also must be constantly aware that anger is one of his tools. His work can stunt or destroy our achievements. Satan tries to defeat us, and make us lose hope. When this evil work of his is also applied to our church body, our attitude of unity makes all the difference. Expose the enemy, fight together, and put your hope in God. Romans 15:13 states, "May the God of hope fill you with all joy and peace in believing, so that by the power of the Holy Spirit you may abound in hope."

Another area that we can draw a comparison in is **sound decision-making**. It comes about through the same three-part process for an individual or for a church. Seeking counsel from the Holy Spirit is first, second is living in God's Word, and understanding His ways, and the third is gaining knowledge and counsel from Godly men and women that are experienced, wise, educated, and care about the end result.

When you have the collective **attitude** of unity in purpose, sound decision-making, hearts surrendered to serve, and leaders that **listen to Jesus,** your church will walk in victory! He will equip your church for battle! Ephesians 4:11-16 states, "And his gifts were that some should be apostles, some prophets, some evangelists, some pastors and teachers, for the equipment of the saints, for the work of ministry, for building up the body of Christ, until we all attain to the unity of the faith and of the knowledge of the Son of God, to mature manhood, to the measure of the stature of the fullness of Christ so that we may no longer be children, tossed to and fro and carried about with every wind of doctrine, by the cunning of men, by their craftiness in deceitful wiles. Rather speaking the truth in love, we are to grow up in every way into him who is the head, into Christ, from whom the whole body, joined and knit together by every joint with which it is supplied, when each part is working properly, makes bodily growth and upbuilds itself in love."

A third area of comparison I would like to mention is the **commission** of an individual that can be paralleled with the **commission** of a church.

There are parts of the Bible I find so exhilarating that I can hardly sit still when I read them. For instance: Every time I read the first and second chapters of Colossians, I have to stop and compose myself because I get so fired up. They fill my mind with a living picture. I am wonderfully overwhelmed with an image of Christians mightily marching forward as they win battle after battle in the war for souls as an army of saints shouting, **"Glory to the Lamb!"** They forge on from battlefield to battlefield; Satan is exposed and suffers defeat after defeat, as God's Kingdom comes to earth in the hearts of mankind! To me these two chapters are a battle song that is trumpeted and sung loudly through the streets of earth, and through the pages of the Bible, marching all the way into Revelation and into heaven! **"Glory to the Lamb!"**

The feeling of victory is sweet! Our knowledge of Revelation, and our God within us assure us that we can claim our victory in Jesus! I was with Mike Tunks and Pastor Peter Shepherd this morning, and as we read these passages, I couldn't contain my excitement. Too bad the rest of the people in the coffee shop didn't understand my joy.

One of the main reasons Paul wrote this Epistle was that the Colossian church had been troubled by the false teachings of Gnosticism. According to various Gnostic Sects and teachers, this world is a result of a primordial error caused by a divine being.

Gnostics believed that they were involved in 'higher thought.' The word Gnostic comes from the Greek word "gnosis," which means knowledge. Their realm of thought included the observance of Jewish holy days and pagan worship days; as well as the worship of Elements of the Universe, and elements of Greek and various Oriental religions.

Paul, guided by the Holy Spirit, set the record straight by writing the truth. In these first two chapters in Colossians, he shows us that Christ is the *ultimate meaning* of the universe; and that salvation through faith in Him is absolute and final. Christ died to reconcile us to the will and purpose of Almighty God!

Please read and study these chapters. I hope you will have the same reaction as I do each time I live in them. Since you are going to read them I'll just put in a couple of highlights.

These are just a few phrases from the first chapter. Colossians 1:4 states, "because we have heard of your faith in Christ Jesus and of the love which you have for all the saints, because of the hope laid up for you in heaven." Verses 9-14 reads, "And so, from the day we heard of it, we have not ceased to pray for you, asking that you may be filled with the knowledge of his will in all spiritual wisdom and understanding, to lead a life worthy of the Lord, fully pleasing to him, bearing fruit in every good work and increasing in the knowledge of God. May you be strengthened with all power, according to his glorious might, for all endurance and patience with joy, giving thanks to the Father, who has qualified us to share in the inheritance of the saints in light. He has delivered us from the dominion of darkness and transferred us to the kingdom of his beloved Son, in whom we have redemption, the forgiveness of sins."

A little farther on in the first chapter Paul talks about the supremacy of Christ. Colossians 1:16-20 tells us, "He is the image of the invisible God, the first-born of all creation; for in him all things were created, in heaven and on earth, visible and invisible, whether thrones or dominions or principalities or authorities--all things were created through him and for him. He is before all things, and in him all things hold together.

He is the head of the body, the church; he is the beginning, the first-born from the dead, that in everything he might be preeminent. For in him all the fullness of God was pleased to dwell, and through him to reconcile to himself all things, whether on earth or in heaven, making peace by the blood of his cross."

We used to be enemies of God, but look at how God sees us now. Colossians 1:21-23 states, "And you, who once were estranged and hostile in mind, doing evil deeds, he has now reconciled in his body of flesh by his death, in order to present you holy and blameless and irreproachable before him, provided that you continue in the faith, stable and steadfast, not shifting from the hope of the gospel which you heard, which has been preached to every creature under heaven, and of which I, Paul, became a minister."

Paul goes on to say that he was commissioned to do his job. From verse 25 we learn, "...I became a minister according to the divine office which was given to me for you, to make the word of God fully known, the mystery hidden for ages and generations but now made manifest to his saints." Paul was commissioned during an appointment with Jesus. Have you been **commissioned** for the work God has called you to do? Have you kept your appointment with Jesus? (Please refer to the next two sections: **Sixteen and Seventeen**, and **The Great**.) If you have, you can then go and be part of a church in which the leaders have kept their appointments with Jesus, and that hears His voice and does His will as you Love God, Love man, and make disciples.

The following passages are excerpts from Colossians, chapter two. Colossians 2:2-3 states, "that their hearts may be encouraged as they are knit together in love, to have all the riches of assured understanding and the knowledge of God's mystery, of Christ, in whom are hid all the treasures of wisdom and knowledge." Colossians 2:8-10 states, "See to it that no one makes a prey of you by philosophy and empty deceit, according to human tradition, according to the elemental spirits of the universe, and not according to Christ. For in Christ all the fullness of deity dwell bodily, and you have come to fullness of life in him, who is the head of all rule and authority." Please take notice of the words **'in him'** which is **'in Jesus.'**

Are you getting excited yet? Colossians 2:11-14 states, "In him also you were circumcised with a circumcision made without hands, by putting off the body of flesh in the circumcision of Christ; and you were buried with him in baptism, in which you were also raised with him through faith in the working of God, who raised him from the dead.

And you, who were dead in trespasses and the uncircumcision of your flesh, God made alive together with him, having forgiven us all our trespasses, having canceled the bond which stood against us with its legal demands; this he set aside, nailing it to the cross." Now look what happened on behalf of those who have life in Jesus! Colossians 2:15 tells us, "He disarmed the principalities and powers and made a public example of them, triumphing over them in him."

May you read and study all that is written in these two chapters, and how they transition into chapter three. Chapter three is about life in Christ, a Holy life. Let Him show you how to move forward in your **commission**. Your life **in Christ** will give you victory!

Each individual Christian can serve God **in** Christ with a life of freedom. As I visit churches that understand the first three chapters of Colossians and the principles of working together in Christ, I hear talk from the pulpit, and from the congregation that is both effective and energizing. This talk and resulting actions lead to success in the war for souls—the Great Commission. Walk in the Son, walk in freedom and victory!

Sixteen and Seventeen

Serving God in the Great Commission has too often been misunderstood since Christ spoke those famous words in Matthew 28:18-20 so long ago. I believe that in the early church, new Christians were taught by word of mouth the importance of what we read in Matthew 28:16-17, which tells us, "Now the eleven disciples went to Galilee, to the mountain to which Jesus had directed them. And when they saw him they worshiped him; but some doubted."

Throughout these past two thousand years, time and money has been dutifully budgeted to construct everything from small, simple places of worship to mammoth, elaborate cathedrals. The Christian faith has been passed on as families taught their children to go to church and await marching orders of going and fighting the war for souls. They lined up in pews or in chairs like soldiers week after week, month after month, year after year until the next generation took over to sit and wait for marching orders. Centuries of church procedure and tradition passed through this important corridor of time; and yet only a few understood how to equip a flock.

Let's uncover the final answers to our mystery in this section and the next one. Please let me point out a crucial word that guides us to understanding the solution. It is found in the direct translation of the original Greek as it states in Matthew 28:16-17, "Now the eleven disciples went to Galilee, to the mountain to which Jesus had directed them. And when they saw him they worshiped him; but some doubted." The word we are focusing on is **appointed**. Moses had an appointment with God. Moses went to the mountain and was commissioned to lead the Israelites to the God who loved them, and to follow in His ways. These eleven disciples had an appointment with Jesus, and he commissioned them to go and make followers of their Lord, and teach them how to walk in His ways, and how to hear his voice.

I believe that each individual and each church must have an appointment with Jesus and surrender their will in order to be commissioned. Go to the mountain before you go to the streets. It doesn't have to be a physical mountain, but can be a symbolic one as you come to Him with a whole-hearted commitment. Keep your appointment and be commissioned by the only One with authority to do so.

The Great...

Matthew 28:18-20 states, "And Jesus came and said to them, 'All authority in heaven and earth has been given to Me. Go therefore and make disciples of all nations, baptizing them in the name of the Father and of the Son and of the Holy Spirit, teaching them to observe all I have commanded you; and lo I am with you always, to the close of the age.'"

As we join our Lord in His work and His Kingdom comes to earth as it is in Heaven, we are commissioned to make disciples of our Lord Christ Jesus. Laboring shoulder-to-shoulder with our brothers and sisters, united in this work, is the most rewarding experience you, or anyone, will ever have. We are to lead people of all nations to Jesus, baptizing them in the name of the Father, the Son, and the Holy Spirit, so they can externally express, and spiritually seal, what is going on internally...this personal relationship with God. We are also to teach them to obey all He has commanded.

Today, Jesus tells us to go and love in His name. He tells us to be not silent. He tells us to be not afraid. See Acts 18:9, Acts 22:16, Mark 16:15, and Galatians 3:26-27.

Moving Forward

Now that I have learned to listen to Him more clearly, I know that He has given me a greater capacity for helping churches to be more effective in fulfilling the Great Commission. I love to talk to people about church growth through winning souls, and now see the benefit of the training He has given me. Until I understood John 15:5, I was not ready, and questions didn't have answers. Now I am confident that He has equipped me to help churches understand and fulfill the Great Commission, and accurately answer most of the questions that arise. This is exciting!

My Savior has told me that it is my job to work with church leaders, and help them learn how to become unified in prayer, thought, and action, so they can effectively reach out into a community with His love and connect with lost souls.

He has taught me that the biggest stumbling block for success in fulfilling the Great Commission is found in the eighteenth verse of the twenty-eighth chapter of Matthew. **All** authority has been given to Jesus. No authority been given to any man or woman unless it comes from Jesus. Failure to deeply understand this one most important fact will cause one to stumble, and sadly fall short of His plan.

My intentions are to continue in the way I used to, and meet with as many pastors and leaders as possible. Now, however, I can truly encourage them in the right direction. Jesus has also provided me with support teams that get involved with each project, and each aspect of this ministry. The support teams are made up of individuals and families that engage in constant prayer, and in some cases, help me with tasks. I also have a group of highly educated and experienced advisors. Through God's grace we are an effective and unified team. This book and our Great Commission help team are tools that we offer to help churches grow with prayer and ideas.

It is evident that many churches need our help simultaneously. As the Lord leads and provides, we will multiply our efforts so that all churches requesting help will get it. We will always offer sound Biblical principles based on God's love to win souls for Christ.

Our Great Commission Help Team has obstacles to overcome. In our agreement with Jesus to serve all Bible-believing churches, we have created a little stir because there are individuals concerned about doctrinal issues. Also, travel today has become very expensive, printing costs are rising, and believers and nonbelievers have an overwhelming amount of temptations and distractions that try to separate them from the Truth.

We invite you to visit the Great Commission Help Center on the internet. You can find us at www.smilingpete.com.

The figures of statistical growth that I listed in the Good News section describe religious identity. We all know that many people identifying themselves as Christian are not members of a church, and have not accepted Jesus into their hearts. It is important that they are included in our outreach.

Our team members are all in agreement with the contents and statements I have written in this book and my opinions, which I believe were guided by the Holy Spirit. If you are also in agreement, and would like to consider joining us, please check the information on our website, www.smilingpete.com. I continually ask the Lord to use the wisdom and gifts that He has given me for the purpose of revealing the Truth, our Lord and Savior, Jesus. To God be all the glory. It is my prayer that I should never boast from my words or in my heart. He sent me here to be a vessel of service. If you choose to join us we will jointly reach out into communities to do His work, supporting our brothers and sisters with prayer and love as we all reach out into a lost world to love God, love man, and make disciples.

Back to the Beginning

Twenty-nine years ago, life for me was miserable and empty. There seemed to be no lasting satisfaction. I fluctuated, back and forth, between a quest for self-fulfillment that couldn't be achieved, and a terrible feeling of being overwhelmed by life's responsibilities.

Every few months I would pick up a note pad and start writing an outline for a book. The title was "Life is a Pressure Cooker." I never got past the outline because it was hard to focus on each problem back then.

One Wednesday night, after a long day of working in Portsmouth, I reached my hand up into the air. I simply said "God, if you are there, I need some help." Months passed.

Two young couples from Mississippi formed a little band. They were talented singers and had all recently been saved. They joined a local Bible-believing church. Jesus sent them, in an old van, on a singing tour to the incarcerated. They evidently stayed in the homes of families in their denomination along the way.

Through a series of incredible circumstances, this little band ended up in my living room, in Concord, New Hampshire, one Saturday afternoon. They told me the salvation story. I had never heard it before.

They told me that Jesus had died on the Cross for me. They said that everyone is a sinner and is separated from God because of sin. However, the Good News is that Jesus' death on the Cross paid the price for my sin to save my soul. His blood paid the penalty so my sins could be washed away. Through confessing I was a sinner, repenting, and accepting Jesus as my own personal Lord and Savior, I could be forgiven and have eternal life with Him. Also, there was other good news, the same *power* that raised Jesus from the dead would come and help me in my life.

This little group of four brand new Christians led me in prayer. "Lord, I confess that I am a sinner. I want to turn from my sins. I believe that Jesus died for my sins on the Cross. I now invite you to come into my heart and life. I accept Jesus as my Lord and Savior, and I will put my trust in Him. Thank you for forgiving me, and for eternal life. Amen."

The kind people from the band then packed up their gear and suggested that I start attending church regularly and join a prayer group. After they left I went into my typical Saturday night routine. I took the kids out for ice cream and later, when they were in bed, I had a few beers and watched TV.

Sunday morning I was in a deep sleep and it took a long time to realize that the doorbell was ringing downstairs. I pulled on a pair of jeans and a t-shirt and ambled down the stairs. As I opened the door I was surprised to see the two guys from the band. They had come to insist that I go to church with them. I first declined, but after they agreed to wait until I brushed my teeth, I decided to go with them. I had never gone to church in jeans before. They were dressed the same, so I went along with the whole idea, and off we went. I was huddled in the back of their van with the band instruments.

We walked into the little Grange Hall just as the service was starting. Before three minutes were up, I thought I was on another planet. As Pastor Steve Earle opened in prayer you could hear people mumbling in agreement, people were raising their hands, a man in the back even yelled out, "Yes Lord!" Then the music started. Some danced, many moved around as they clapped to the beat of the music. There were shouts of praise while emotion flowed all over the room in this strange world. Pastor Earle had enthusiasm and smiled almost constantly. People sang and laughed and raised their hands as they praised God.

The music stopped and the congregation greeted each other as they left their seats and wandered all over the room for handshakes and hugs. I was overwhelmed by their genuine friendliness as they extended outstretched hands and big smiles. Most of them told me their names and wanted to know mine. The sermon was different from anything I had ever heard. It was as if the pastor was assuming that Jesus was in us. The strangest thing is that before half the service was over I felt comfortable, very comfortable.

The band members were brand new Christians and were doing the job that their Savior had assigned them. They didn't know a lot about the Bible but they knew Jesus, and they knew about the enemy, and understood that only about one in four surrenders a whole heart when accepting Jesus. Without a totally surrendered heart one is not truly born again. If they hadn't taken me to church there is a seventy-five percent chance that the devil would have devoured me, and stolen my salvation. Please study Luke 8: 1-18.

Later that same day I walked into the woods and said the sinner's prayer again, but this time I lifted up an undivided heart to Him in surrender. At that moment I passed from death to life, in Christ... forever.

By the way, that was twenty-nine years ago. Pastor Earle is still preaching and smiling (in another area of the state), and I'm just getting warmed up in telling a lost world about my Savior.

Going…

Together, we Christians are to fight the war for souls. We are to be united in glorifying our God and lifting up our Savior as we love God, love man, and make disciples. We are to be humble servants in one accord. In my opinion it is far more important (and effective) to lead souls to Christ by loving and serving them rather than by dictating doctrine. They can't hear the doctrine until they have been loved and served by the love of Christ in us, and unless God draws them.

I have spent years traveling about and interviewing people from all walks of life. I have stood on street corners, outside malls, outside supermarkets, outside bars, at sporting events, at political rallies, in camping facilities, and anywhere else I could find people; and have talked to them about my Savior and about the Christian church. Too many lost souls have described a negative attitude toward those who are supposed to represent Christ. I have heard over and over, "They hate me because of who I am."

As the writing of this book came to a close, I realized that I was under a spiritual attack stronger than I had ever experienced. All phases of my life started reeling. I was constantly uncomfortable and never at peace. Several of my relationships went haywire, work became a nightmare, and nothing seemed right.

Reading my notes on spiritual warfare led me to believe that the answer was in Christ, but I just didn't get it. I asked my friends, clergy, and members of my home group to pray. Weeks passed. I was miserable. Down on my knees, I told my Savior I couldn't take much more. Then it happened. I started getting daily emails from Jann telling me that the answer is to love and forgive.

On the third night, after printing out her emails and praying, I had a dream about Christ suffering on the Cross. He showed me how

He forgave those who had done such horrible things to Him. He took me through the fall, and helped me understand how the enemy enters into people and tries to destroy them. It is hard to describe how close I was to Jesus in the dream. It was almost like I was over His left shoulder, but He was in my mind showing me what He wanted me to see, not with words, but a vision and an unspoken understanding. The first thing I realized was that it was gradually getting darker. Next, right in front of me was the unmistakable, deep, dark, lush greenery of the Garden of Eden. The last rays of sunlight highlighted the fruit. Then came the knowledge of forgiveness and how He defeated the enemy with His blood.

It was about four in the morning when I sat up in bed. I was barely half awake when hidden scrolls of unforgiveness were unveiled. I became acutely aware of specific individuals who had wronged me and I was neither forgiving nor loving them. I confessed my sin and forgave these people from a place in my heart that had not previously existed. Victory in Jesus was swift. I could immediately feel the absence of evil forces. Daylight came and led into a morning of reconciliation. I went in person to forgive the ones who had wronged me. Jesus went ahead of me and softened their hearts before I arrived. God truly is love. My closeness and trust in Him have greatly increased.

Now I have a better comprehension of what it means to live in Christ and am better able to tap that vein of divine power to go and love, and live in His peace. I am thankful for the wisdom Jesus has given me about spiritual warfare through answered prayer, through the pastors' sermons in my new church, and through caring, fellow Christians. I am also thankful that after almost thirty years of walking with Him, my sanctification is in His hands. Each step amazes me. The continual transformation, through which we surrender to God, gradually leads us to develop the strengths of His character, enabling us to accomplish our mission. Our souls need to heal from the fall, not partially, but fully, through a deeper filling of Jesus at each stage of growth.

May the God of Jacob bless and keep you. Psalm 138:7-8 assures us that He is always with us as we live in His plan. It states, "Though I walk in the midst of trouble, thou dost preserve my life; thou dost stretch out thy hand against the wrath of my enemies, and thy right hand delivers me. The Lord will fulfil his purpose for me; thy steadfast love, O Lord, endures for ever. Do not forsake the work of thy hands."

May you succeed in your journey and someday realize oceans of rewards.

Peter Carver Johnson
"Smiling Pete"

References

Scripture quotations are from the Revised Standard Version of the Bible, copyright © 1946, 1952, and 1971 by the National Council of the Churches of Christ in the U.S.A. Used by permission. All rights reserved.

Original Greek to English translations obtained from:

Interlinear Greek-English New Testament, George Ricker Berry, Baker Books, Grand Rapids, 1897. 2003 (25th printing). Pages 18, 38, 78, 147.

John Wesley: A Biography, Stephen Tomkins, Wm. B. Eerdmans Publishing Company Grand Rapids/Cambridge, 2003. Pages 48-51.

National Geographic, December 2007 Edition, National Geographic, Washington, D.C., Page 114.

The Holy Spirit & Power, Editor: Dr. Larry Keefauver, Bridge-Logos, Gainesville, 2003. Pages 48-51.

A Glimpse into Glory, Kathryn Kuhlman with Jamie Buckingham, Bridge-Logos, 1983. Pages 66.

Victory in Jesus and The Lord's Healing Touch, Kathryn Kuhlman, Kathryn Kuhlman Foundation. Pages 63.

Zondervan Bible Comparison Guide, Page 111. Zondervan, Grand Rapids, MI 49530, Page 112.

Webster's New Collegiate Dictionary G. & C. Merriam Co. 1981.

NKJV Exhaustive Concordance Thomas Nelson Publishers, Nashville, 1992.

The Abingdon Bible Commentary Abingdon Press, New York-Nashville, 1929.

The Westminster Dictionary of Christian Theology The Westminster Press, Philadelphia, 1983.

Calvary's Cross, The Bible Institute Colportage Association of Chicago, 1900. Page 124.

Kathryn Kuhlman: A Spiritual Biography of God's Miracle Working Power, Roberts Liardon, Harrison House, Inc., Tulsa, 1990. Page 85.

Sermons cited are from Grace Capital Church, Pembroke, NH

Recommended Reading

"House To House" by Larry Kreider,
Touch Publications, 1995

"A Glimpse Into Glory" by Kathryn Kuhlman with Jamie Buckingham,
Bridge-Logos, 1983

"I Believe In Miracles" by Kathryn Kuhlman
Kathryn Kuhlman Foundation, 1992

"The Holy Spirit and Power" by John Wesley,
Bridge-Logos, 2003

"The Potential Principle" by Edwin Louis Cole,
Whitaker House, 1984

"The Journal, God's Word Applied"
www.foursquare.org

Please visit us at:

www.gchcenter.com
www.smilingpete.com

Glossary of Terms and Names

Accept Jesus   God's kindom comes to earth in your heart and soul when you accept Jesus as your Lord and Savior, and God becomes more than your Creator, He becomes your Heavenly Father in a relationship that will last forever.

Atonement   The reconciliation of God and man through the sacrificial death of Christ Jesus.

Bible-believing church   A church whose leadership, doctrine, and mindset agree that one must obtain direction, understanding-knowledge, expression of faith, history of God's works, and the narrative itself as guided by the Holy Spirit, from the Bible. A church that strives to always seek the Truth, the Person Christ Jesus, and in all things commit their hearts and will to Him in complete surrender. A church whose members believe that the Bible is the living Word of God.

Born Again   The act of being born again is the joining to God, birthing process that is made possible by the blood that Christ sacrificed for you on the Cross—in atonement for your sins. As you confess that you are a sinner and accept Christ as your Lord and Savior the blood that Jesus shed for you is so powerful that you are cleansed, you are forgiven. When you truly lift up your heart, soul, and will to Him in surrender forever the birthing is complete and in a moment you become a child... of God, and He becomes your Father.

When one is born again they are delivered from the spiritual dimension that the devil controls and are connected to God's Spirit...forever.

Convert   One who has changed from one faith to another; especially one who has become a Christian.

Doctrine   The belief, or system of beliefs, of a group.

Evangelism   The winning or revival of personal commitments to Christ.

Expiation   The act of making atonement.

Flock   A group under the guidance of a leader; *specif:* a church congregation in relation to the pastor.

God's Plan   God's plan for each of us is to have a close, personal relationship with Him that grows and lasts forever. He is Love and He is Holy. He created all of us for His pleasure. When you accept Christ as your Lord and Savior you begin a love affair with God that will never end. God's plan glorifies our Lord and Savior, Jesus.

Great Commission   Matthew 28:18-20 "And Jesus came and said to them, 'All authority in heaven and on earth has been given to me. Go therefore and make disciples of all nations, baptizing them in the name of the Father and of the Son and of the Holy Spirit, teaching them to observe all that I have commanded you; and lo, I am with you always, to the close of the age.' "

Holy Spirit   The Holy Spirit is the third Person in the Godhead or Trinity. The Holy Spirit is the active presence of God in human life.

Home Groups   Home groups (sometimes called small groups, home prayer groups, fellowship groups, cell groups, etc.) meet weekly for prayer and study. Outreach is a natural extension of home groups as members witness to, pray for, and invite their neighbors to join in the group and the church.

In Christ   When you are born again you are joined [forever alive] to God in Christ Jesus our Lord and are dead to sin. As you learn to surrender your will to God, who molds you to be more like Christ, you will be guided by the indwelling of the Holy Spirit. Romans 3:23 tells us, "For the wages of sin is death, but the free gift of God is eternal life in Christ Jesus our Lord."

Intercessor   A Christian who prays for others. See Romans 8:26-27, Romans 8:34, and Hebrews 7:25 to understand divine intercession.

Lamb   A lamb was often offered as a sacrifice to God in the Old Testament. Jesus became the sacrificial Lamb of God by dying on the Cross in the New Testament.

Power of the Cross   Jesus' death on the Cross was so powerful that in a moment His blood reconciled mankind to God, so that all who accept Him as Lord and Savior will be joined to God and have eternal life in heaven.

Propitiation   An atoning sacrifice.

Rector   A rector is simply a minister. In a church with several ministers he is what we might call the senior pastor. In Wesley's day most churches were small and usually had a rector without associates or staff.

Resurrection   The rising of Christ from the dead three days after His death on the Cross is celebrated annually as Easter by Christians. He is now eternally seated at the right hand of the Father.

Sanctification   Sanctification is the life-long molding process that begins when you are born again. God will transform you into a new creature in Christ. Old desires and ideals will gradually pass away and His righteous ways will become yours as you become more like Christ. The process is completed when you enter heaven.

Satan   The Hebrew word 'Satan' means adversary. By New Testament description, he is the lord and leader of evil spirits who oppose God and oppress men. We learn from the New Testament that he, the devil, is out to destroy us.

Saved   God loves us so much that He sacrificed His Son, the only Righteous One, for us on the Cross, so that if we accept Jesus as our Lord and Savior, we receive eternal life (also called salvation) and are 'saved' forever. Being saved means that our sins are forgiven and we are no longer separated from God. It means we will be spared from the wrath of God, which otherwise leads to the second death on Judgment day. We are saved by His grace, receiving not the death we deserve, but eternal life. We are also saved to fulfill the unique purpose for which He created each of us.

Sin   The breaking of God's code of conduct which caused the separation of man from God.

Sinner's Prayer   The Sinner's prayer is a prayer of surrender that comes from your heart when you desire to be born again. It is your intention that is important and not the exact wording. When you talk to Almighty God with this prayer, your will must be humbled and you must desire to serve Him instead of yourself…forever.

This is a prayer that is often prayed "Lord, I confess that I am a sinner. I want to turn from my sins. I believe that Jesus died for my sins on the Cross. I now invite You to come into my heart and life. I accept Jesus as my Lord and Savior, and I will put my trust in Him. Thank you for forgiving me, and for the gift of eternal life. Amen."

Spiritual Warfare   The war against evil. We constantly fight against the enemy of our souls, the devil who is a spirit.

Supplication   Also known as petitioning, this is a type of prayer where one asks God to provide something, either for themselves or for someone else.

Trinity   God the Father, the Son (or Word), and the Holy Spirit are the three Persons of the Godhead.

Witnessing   When led by the Holy Spirit, the act of sharing with others about the love in one's heart for God and man, eternal salvation through Christ, and of the joy and peace of serving since being born again.

John Wesley (1703-1791)   John Wesley, an Anglican minister and evangelist who had an enormous influence on modern Christianity, including his role as founding father of the Methodists. He preached that you must be born anew and led the first widely successful evangelical movement in England.

Kathryn Kuhlman (1907-1976)   Kathryn Kuhlman believed in miracles and taught that you must be born again. Though proclaimed a faith healer by the news media, she denied any special powers, and gave all glory to God. There are more documented healings involved with her ministry than any other except the Bible. She explained that it was the power of the Holy Spirit that healed people. Her love and relationship with Jesus was victorious.

Aimee Semple McPherson (1890-1944)   Aimee Semple McPherson preached that Jesus was and is the same yesterday and today and forever. (Hebrews 13:8). She was also labeled a faith healer and gave all glory to God. She started the Foursquare movement.

Printed in the United States
204074BV00004B/1-51/P